HCG Cookbook

Book Decsription

Thank you for downloading my HCG Diet Plan Cookbook for Weight Loss. Boasting several recipes to try during your Phase 2 of the HCG weight loss diet program, this book is all you need. All my recipes are healthy, interesting and delicious.

I personally like the HCG program and the outcome I have noted since I tried it. I have lost a lot of fat within a short period of time. I never thought I would ever be thin again; the HCG weight loss program has completely changed my life.

By losing the fat I had previously, the HCG plan has done more than make my body look smaller. In addition to this, the diet has affected my cholesterol and blood pressure levels in a positive way. My blood glucose levels are more favorable than ever before and I cannot be happier.

All the same, I have had to get more creative with the way I select my food because the program offers limited choices. This has helped me avoid boredom from eating the same type of food all the time. That's why I have remained actively involved in the program.

In an attempt to create a broader food list, I have gathered the following recipes that could keep your eating program fun, appetizing and awesome. If you follow my recipes, you will stay longer on your HCG diet program. For the moment, I honestly and sincerely wish you good luck.

Table of Contents

The HCG Diet Plan

So what exactly is the HCG diet plan and what makes it extremely special and effective? The plan entails the use of a cautiously planned diet of good quality healthy food and a tiny amount of the HCG hormone. The hormone is mainly administered via drops or injections. Dr Simeons' rigid protocol that offered limited flexibility, a specific food list and no exercise recommendations is no longer fully in use. The HCG diet has greatly evolved into a few contemporary protocols.

The plans available today recommend a low-calorie diet with a longer food list than the former one. The HCG diet plan is more than just a means of cutting excess weight. It can be described as a medical hormone therapy created to re-program a dieter's metabolism and eating habits. HCG is only used to alter the way we lose weight and to set us on the path of long-term fitness and health.

The Seven-Day HCG Diet Meal Plan

Day	Breakfast	AM SNACK	Lunch	PM SNACK	Dinner	BEDTIME SNACK
Phase One (Day One & Two) During this phase, eat and drink everything and anything you want but make sure you: • Drink at least 8 glasses of water per day • Drink apple cider vinegar everyday						
Day 1	1 Serving Orange Strawberry Smoothie	1 Serving Dreamy Fruit Cup	1 Serving Hot Chicken Curry + Melba Toast	1 serving Tasty Fruity Salad	1 Serving Mushroom Fish Filet +	1 Glass (250 ml) Hot Apple Cider
Day 2	1 Serving Chocolate Toffee Coffee Smoothie	1 Serving Frozen Cocoa Strawberries	1 Serving Ground Beef Tacos	1 Serving Dark Chocolate Flavored Orange Slices	1 Serving Roasted Beef Brisket + Strawberry & Cucumber Salad	1 Glass (250 ml) Hot Apple Cider

Phase Two (Day Three & Onwards)

During this phase, strictly adhere to the meal plan, drinking green tea, chamomile tea and yerba mate. Do not take any other tea! Also take coffee without sugar (use stevia to sweeten your tea or coffee). Remember to drink at least 8 glasses of water per day

Day	Breakfast	AM SNACK	Lunch	PM SNACK	Dinner	BEDTIME SNACK
Day 3	1 Cup Hot Coffee	1 Serving Sorbet 'de Strawberry	1 Serving Ground Beef Chili + 1 Serving Red Cabbage Salad+ 1 Apple	1 Serving Strawberry Sorbet	1 Serving Poached Halibut + Orange Cucumber Salad + 1 Grapefruit	1 Glass (250ml) Orange-Ade
Day 4	1 Cup Hot Green Tea	1 Serving Lemon Pops	1 Serving Cabbage-Orange Salad w/ Chicken + 1 Pear	1 Serving Apple & Strawberry Snack	1 Serving Sweet Ginger Shrimp + Spicy Thai-Style Cucumber Salad _ 1 Apple	1 Glass (250ml) Bloody Hot Thin Mary
Day 5	1 Cup Coffee	1 Serving Melba Toast w/ Strawberry Jam	1 Serving Spiced Chicken Salad + 1 Apple	1 Serving Apple Chips	1 Serving Sweet & Crunchy Apple Chicken Salad	1 Glass (250ml) Fresh and Feisty Strawberry Lemonade
Day 6	1 Cup Hot Green Tea	1 Serving Spicy Frozen Orange Slices	1 Serving Fennel Citrus Salad + 1 Serving Roasted Beef Brisket + 1 Banana	1 Serving Apple Candy	1 Serving Cabbage-Orange Salad w/ Chicken + 1 Apple	1 Glass (250ml) 1 Glass (250ml) Orange-Ade
Day 7	1 Cup Hot Coffee	1 Serving Toast with Spicy Cucumber	1 Serving Tasty Japanese Cucumber Salad + Italian Veal + 1 Apple	1 Serving Apple Slices w/ Cinnamon Sauce	1 Serving Oven-Fried Chicken Tenders + Curried Celery Salad	1 Glass (250ml) Fresh and Feisty Strawberry Lemonade

Phase Three(The Maintenance Phase)

This is a six weeks long phase, where you'll eat healthy avoiding starches and sugars during the first three weeks and slowly adding them back into your diet during the last three weeks. Good Luck!

HCG Soups, Broths & Stews

Tasty Basil-Tomato Soup

Yield: 2 Servings
Total Time: 40 Minutes
Prep Time: 10 Minutes
Cook Time: 30 Minutes

Ingredients

- 2 cups chicken broth
- 2 tablespoons chopped onion
- 2 cloves garlic, minced
- 3 ounces tomato paste
- 2 cups diced tomatoes
- 6 leaves fresh basil, chopped
- ¼ teaspoon dried oregano
- 1 teaspoon garlic powder
- Pinch of marjoram
- Pinch of Salt
- Pinch of black pepper

Directions:

In a food processor, process all ingredients until smooth; transfer to a saucepan and bring to a gentle boil. Lower heat and simmer for about 20-30 minutes. Serve hot garnished with parsley or basil.

Puree all ingredients in a food processor or blender. Pour into a saucepan

Nutritional Information per Serving:

Calories: 288; Total Fat: 4.8 g; Carbs: 17.2 g; Dietary Fiber: 4.4 g; Sugars: 10.7 g; Protein: 44.4 g; Cholesterol: 108 mg; Sodium: 140 mg

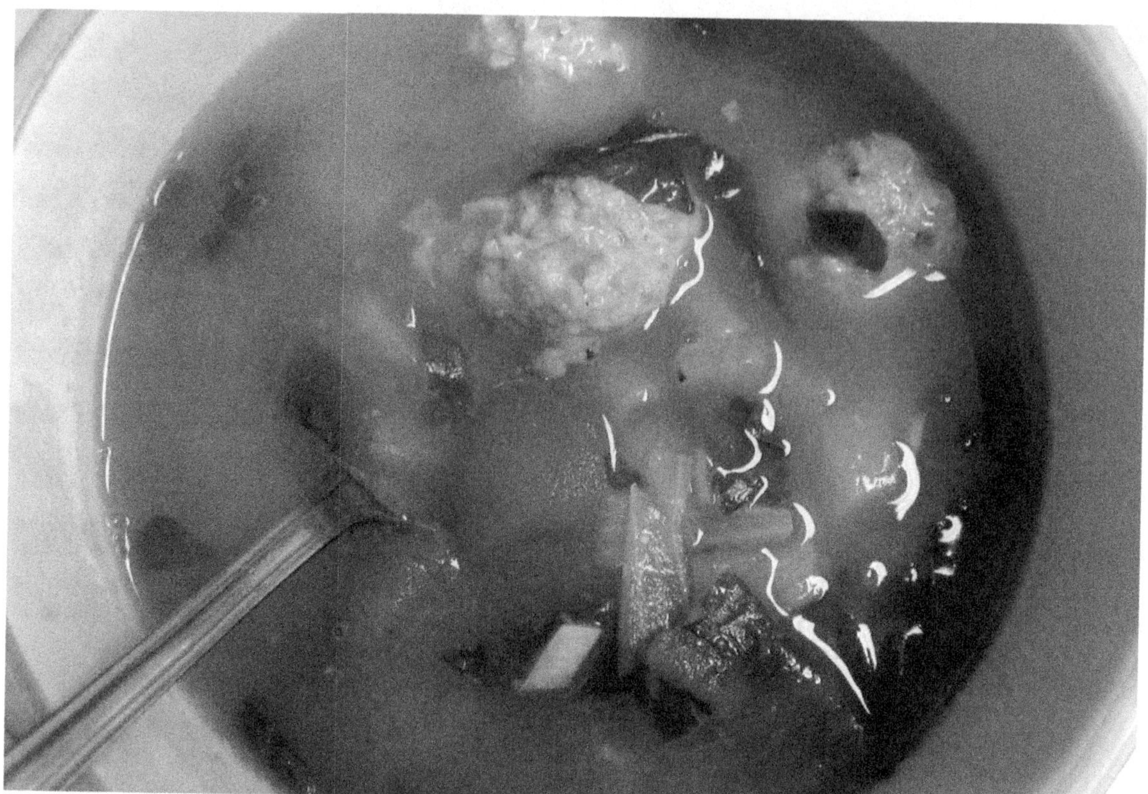

Scrumptious Chicken Meatball Soup

Yield: 1 Serving
Total Time: 40 Minutes
Prep Time: 10 Minutes
Cook Time: 30 Minutes

Ingredients

For Meatballs

- 100 grams chicken breast, ground
- 1 red onion, minced
- 1 clove garlic, minced
- Dash of garlic powder
- Dash of onion powder
- Pinch of thyme
- Pinch of marjoram
- Pinch of sage
- ½ cup whole wheat bread crumbs, optional

Broth

- 2 cups chicken broth
- 1 tablespoon apple cider vinegar
- 2 tablespoons Bragg's liquid aminos
- 2 cloves garlic, minced
- 1 tablespoon chopped red onion
- Chopped celery
- 1 bay leaf
- Pinch of cayenne pepper
- Pinch of salt
- Pinch of black pepper

Directions:

In a bowl, mix together chicken, crushed Melba toast, onion, garlic and spices; form meatballs from the mixture.

In a saucepan, bring broth to a gentle boil; stir in vinegar, liquid aminos, spices and chicken balls. Lower heat and simmer for at least 30 minutes. Add tomato or celery during the last 5 minutes of cooking.

Nutritional Information per Serving:

Calories: 208; Total Fat: 3.8 g; Carbs: 7.7 g; Dietary Fiber: 1.3 g; Sugars: 3.9 g; Protein: 39.3 g; Cholesterol: 63 mg; Sodium: 3500 mg

Beefy Vegetable Soup

Yield: 1 Serving
Total Time: 45 Minutes
Prep Time: 10 Minutes
Cook Time: 35 Minutes

Ingredients

- 2 cups beef
- 100 grams lean beef, diced
- 1 tablespoon chopped onion
- 1 clove garlic, minced
- 3 stalks celery, diced
- 1 bay leaf
- 1/8 teaspoon dried oregano
- 1/8 teaspoon dried basil
- Pinch of chili powder
- Pinch of paprika
- Pinch of thyme
- Pinch of salt
- Pinch of black pepper

Directions:

In a saucepan, mix beef, celery, garlic, onion, broth and spices and simmer for about 20-30 minutes; stir in tomatoes and simmer for 5 minutes more.

Phase 3 modifications: Add more veggies such as bell peppers, zucchini or chopped carrots.

Nutritional Information per Serving:

Calories: 199; Total Fat: 6.4 g; Carbs: 2.7 g; Dietary Fiber: 1.2 g; Sugars: 1 g; Protein: 30.9 g; Cholesterol: 89 mg; Sodium: 102 mg

Savory Chicken Soup

Yield: 1 Serving
Total Time: 30 Minutes
Prep Time: 10 Minutes
Cook Time: 20 Minutes

Ingredients

- 100 grams chicken breast, diced
- 2 cups tomatoes, chopped
- 2 cups chicken broth
- 1 red onion, minced
- 2 cloves garlic, chopped
- ½ teaspoon poultry spice blend
- 1 bay leaf
- Pinch of cayenne pepper
- Pinch of salt
- Pinch of black pepper

Directions:

Add chicken broth to a pan and bring to a boil; stir in garlic, onion, chicken, vegetables, and spices. Simmer for about 20 minutes or until cabbage and chicken are cooked through. Serve hot sprinkled with parsley of chives.

Nutritional Information per Serving:

Calories: 228; Total Fat: 5.7 g; Carbs: 9.9 g; Dietary Fiber: 2.5 g; Sugars: 6.6 g; Protein: 32.8 g; Cholesterol: 64 g; Sodium: 1587 mg

Thai- Style Beef Soup

Yield: 1 Serving
Total Time: 40 Minutes
Prep Time: 10 Minutes
Cook Time: 30 Minutes

Ingredients

- 100 grams lean beef
- 1 tablespoon chopped green onion
- 1 clove garlic, minced
- 1 stalk celery
- 3 tablespoons Bragg's liquid aminos
- 2 cups beef broth
- 1 bay leaf
- Handful fresh cilantro
- 1/8 teaspoon red pepper flakes
- ½ teaspoon fresh grated ginger
- Pinch of cinnamon
- Pinch of stevia
- Pinch of salt
- Pinch of pepper

Directions:

Add broth to a pot and bring to a boil; stir in onion, garlic, Bragg's, spices and bay leaf; return to a boil and then lower heat; simmer for about 5 minutes and add celery and beef. Cook for about 20-30 minutes or until beef is tender; season with stevia, salt and pepper. Serve garnished with chopped cilantro.

Phase 3 modifications: add sesame oil or chili and a handful of bean sprouts to soup and serve topped with sliced mushrooms.

Nutritional Information per Serving:

Calories: 272; Total Fat: 9.1 g; Carbs: 3.9 g; Dietary Fiber: 0.8 g; Sugars: 0.8 g; Protein: 40.4 g; Cholesterol: 89 mg; Sodium: 1611 mg

Healthy Chicken Broth

Yield: 6 Servings
Total Time: 4 Hours 35 Minutes
Prep Time: 10 Minutes
Cook Time: 4 Hours 5 Minutes

Ingredients

- 3 large chicken breasts
- ½ large red onion, chopped
- 5 cloves garlic, finely chopped
- 4 stalks celery, chopped
- 10 cups water
- 1 bay leaf
- Pinch of salt
- Pinch of pepper

Directions:

Combine chicken and water in a soup pot; stir in spices and celery and bring to a gentle boil. Lower heat and simmer for about 4 hours; remove chicken and veggies from broth. Place broth in the fridge; skim off and strain through affine mesh for a clear stock. Use chicken to prepare chicken salad (page 43).

Nutritional Information per Serving:

Calories: 180; Total Fat: 6 g; Carbs: 9.1 g; Dietary Fiber: 2.7 g; Sugars: 4.1 g; Protein: 22.4 g; Cholesterol: 65 mg; Sodium: 120 mg

Healthy Vegetable Broth

Yield: 4-6 Servings
Total Time: 4 Hours 5 Minutes
Prep Time: 10 Minutes
Cook Time: 4 Hours 5 Minutes

Ingredients

- 10 cups water
- ½ large red onion, chopped
- 10 cloves garlic, chopped
- 2 bay leaves
- 10 stalks celery
- 1 teaspoon thyme
- 1 teaspoon basil
- 1 teaspoon garlic powder
- 1 teaspoon paprika
- Pinch of salt
- Pinch of pepper

Directions:

In a large pot, bring water to a rolling boil; sir in spices and veggies and slow cook for about 2-4 hours. Strain out the veggies and cool; use the veggies as a base for soups.

Nutritional Information per Serving:

Calories: 65; Total Fat: 0.6 g; Carbs: 4 g; Dietary Fiber: 4.7 g; Sugars: 5.5 g; Protein: 2.4 g; Cholesterol: 0 mg; Sodium: 87 mg

Spicy Fennel Soup

Yield: 1 Serving
Total Time: 30 Minutes
Prep Time: 10 Minutes
Cook Time: 20 Minutes

Ingredients

- 2 cups chicken
- 3 fennel bulbs, chopped
- ¼ teaspoon allspice seasoning
- 1 tablespoon minced onion
- Pinch of salt
- Pinch of pepper

Directions:

In a small saucepan set over low heat, combine vegetable broth, minced onion, spices, chopped fennel bulbs and simmer for about 20 minutes; stir in lemon rind and serve warm garnished with chopped fennel sprigs.

Phase 3 modifications: Add cream or half and half to the soup.

Nutritional Information per Serving:

Calories: 108; Total Fat: 2.9 g; Carbs: 9.2 g; Dietary Fiber: 2.9 g; Sugars: 1.8 g; Protein: 10.9 g; Cholesterol: 0 mg; Sodium: 572 mg

Tasty Celery Soup

Yield: 1 Serving
Total Time: 40 Minutes
Prep Time: 10 Minutes
Cook Time: 30 Minutes

Ingredients

- 2 cups chicken broth
- ¼ teaspoon dried basil
- ¼ teaspoon thyme
- 3 stalks celery
- 1 bay leaf
- Pinch of salt
- Pinch of pepper

Directions:

Cook celery until tender; transfer to a blender and add in spices and broth; blend until smooth. Return to pan and simmer for about 20-30 minutes.

Nutritional Information per Serving:

Calories: 81; Total Fat: 2.8 g; Carbs: 2.6 g; Dietary Fiber: 0.4 g; Sugars: 1.6 g; Protein: 9.9 g; Cholesterol: 0 mg; Sodium: 1540 mg

Ground Beef Chili

Yield: 1 Serving
Total Time: 35 Minutes
Prep Time: 10 Minutes
Cook Time: 25 Minutes

Ingredients

- 100 grams lean ground beef
- 1 tablespoon chopped red onion
- 2 cloves garlic, minced
- 1 cup chopped tomatoes
- ½ cup water
- Pinch of garlic powder
- ¼ teaspoon chili powder
- Pinch of oregano
- Pinch of onion powder
- Pinch of cayenne pepper
- Pinch of salt
- Pinch of pepper

Directions:

In a small frying pan, cook beef until browned; stir in garlic, onion, tomatoes, water and spices and simmer for a few minutes or until liquid is reduced, adding water as needed. Season with salt and pepper and serve garnished with chopped tomato or green onion.

Phase 3 modifications: Top with a dollop of sour cream or cheddar cheese.

Nutritional Information per Serving:

Calories: 227; Total Fat: 6.7 g; Carbs: 9 g; Dietary Fiber: 5.4 g; Sugars: 2.8 g; Protein: 32.2 g; Cholesterol: 89 mg; Sodium: 86 mg

Lemony Chicken & Spinach Soup

Yield: 1 Serving
Total Time: 40 Minutes
Prep Time: 10 Minutes
Cook Time: 30 Minutes

Ingredients

- 100 grams chicken
- 2 cups chopped spinach
- 2 cups chicken broth
- ½ lemon with rind
- 1 clove garlic, minced
- 1 tablespoon chopped red onion
- 1 stalk lemongrass
- ¼ teaspoon thyme
- Pinch of cayenne pepper
- Pinch of salt & pepper

Directions:

In a small saucepan brown chicken in a splash of fresh lemon juice; stir in garlic, onion, spices, broth, lemon juice and lemon rind and simmer for about 20-30 minutes, adding spinach during the last 5 minutes. Serve hot.

Nutritional Information per Serving:

Calories: 240; Total Fat: 6 g; Carbs: 4.2 g; Dietary Fiber: 1.1 g; Sugars: 2 g; Protein: 39.7 g; Cholesterol: 77 mg; Sodium: 1614 mg

Asparagus Soup

Yield: 1 Serving
Total Time: 15 Minutes
Prep Time: 5 Minutes
Cook Time: 10 Minutes

Ingredients

- 4-5 stalks asparagus, tough ends removed
- 1 tablespoon milk
- 2 tablespoons chopped onion
- 3 tablespoons Bragg's liquid aminos
- 2 cups chicken broth
- ¼ teaspoon thyme
- ¼ teaspoon onion powder
- ¼ teaspoon garlic powder
- Pinch of Old Bay seasoning
- Pinch of salt & pepper
- 1 bay leaf

Directions:

Steam asparagus until tender; transfer to a food processor along with broth and spices and puree until smooth. Heat in a saucepan and serve.

Variation: add 100g of diced chicken to the soup. Use 1-2 Old Bay seasonings instead of dried spices.

Phase 3 modifications: melt butter and sauté onion; stir in sliced mushrooms, half and half or cheddar cheese to soup.

Nutritional Information per Serving:

Calories: 111; Total Fat: 3.2 g; Carbs: 8.1 g; Dietary Fiber: 2 g; Sugars: 4.5 g; Protein: 12 g; Cholesterol: 1 mg; Sodium: 1616 mg

Hot & Sour Chicken Soup

Yield: 1 Serving
Total Time: 45 Minutes
Prep Time: 10 Minutes
Cook Time: 35 Minutes

Ingredients

- 100 grams chicken breast diced
- 2 tablespoons chopped red onion
- 1 clove garlic, minced
- ½ lemon quarters with rind
- 1 cup chicken broth
- 4 tablespoons Bragg's liquid aminos
- 4 tablespoons apple cider vinegar
- 1 cup water
- Pinch of Cayenne pepper
- Pinch of red chili flakes
- Pinch of salt & pepper
- Pinch of stevia

Directions:

Add a cup of water to a saucepan and boil lemon rind and wedges until pulp comes off the rind. Squeeze out lemon juice from wedges and additional pulp from rind and discard the wedges and rind; stir in chicken broth, diced chicken and spices and simmer until chicken is cooked through.

Variation: add orange juice to the soup plus your favorite veggies. Use shrimp instead of chicken.

Phase 3 modifications: add a splash of pineapple juice and veggies such as carrots, cauliflower, zucchini, etc. for added flavor and heat, add a little chili or paste to soup.

Nutritional Information per Serving:

Calories: 175; Total Fat: 4 g; Carbs: 3.7 g; Dietary Fiber: 0.62 g; Sugars: 1.8 g; Protein: 26.4 g; Cholesterol: 64 mg; Sodium: 829 mg

Creole Gumbo with Shrimp

Yield: 1 Serving
Total Time: 40 Minutes
Prep Time: 10 Minutes
Cook Time: 30 Minutes

Ingredients

- 100 grams shrimp
- Dash of Worcestershire sauce
- 3 tablespoons apple cider vinegar
- 2 cups vegetable broth
- 2 tablespoons chopped green onion
- 2 cloves of garlic, minced
- 3 tablespoons tomato paste
- 2 tomatoes, chopped
- Cayenne pepper
- Salt and pepper
- Liquid smoke hickory smoke flavoring

Directions:

Sauté onions in a saucepan and stir in shrimp of chicken sausage; fry until cooked through and then stir in vinegar, broth, spices, tomatoes and tomato paste. Simmer for about 20-30 minutes and serve hot garnished with chopped parsley.

Phase 3 modifications: add more protein like sausage, chicken and grab plus additional veggies such as bell peppers, celery and okra. Serve topped with a dollop of sour cream.

Nutritional Information per Serving:

Calories: 248; Total Fat: 4.7.4 g; Carbs: 13.7g; Dietary Fiber: 2.3 g; Sugars: 7.6 g; Protein: 34.7 g; Cholesterol: 211 mg; Sodium: 1830 mg

Middle Eastern-Style Veggie Soup

Yield: 1 Serving
Total Time: 40 Minutes
Prep Time: 10 Minutes
Cook Time: 30 Minutes

Ingredients

- 2 cups vegetable broth
- Tomatoes chopped or celery
- 8 ounces tomato sauce
- 1 clove garlic, minced
- 1 tablespoon chopped onion
- 1/8 teaspoon ginger, crushed
- ¼ teaspoon cumin
- Pinch of salt and black pepper
- Fresh mint, cilantro or parsley

Directions:

In a saucepan, mix tomato paste, tomato sauce and broth; bring to a gentle boil. Lower heat and simmer for about 20-30 minutes or until veggies are tender.

Phase 3 modifications: add zucchini, string beans or any of your favorite veggies.

Nutritional Information per Serving:

Calories: 138; Total Fat: 3.3 g; Carbs: 15.4 g; Dietary Fiber: 3.7 g; Sugars: 11.5 g; Protein: 12.9 g; Cholesterol: 0 mg; Sodium: 2713 mg

Crab Bisque

Yield: 1 Serving
Total Time: 40 Minutes
Prep Time: 10 Minutes
Cook Time: 30 Minutes

Ingredients

- 100 grams crab meat
- 1 tablespoon minced onion
- 1 clove garlic, minced
- 1 tablespoon milk
- 2 cups vegetable broth
- 1 cup chopped tomatoes
- 1 teaspoon Old Bay seasoning
- Pinch of cayenne pepper
- Pinch of salt & pepper
- 1 bay leaf

Directions:

In a food processor, combine broth and tomatoes and puree; transfer to a saucepan and heat. Stir in spices and crab and simmer, stirring frequently, for about 20-30 minutes.

Phase 3 modifications: add cream or half and half.

Nutritional Information per Serving:

Calories: 216; Total Fat: 5.3 g; Carbs: 13.5; Dietary Fiber: 2.5 g; Sugars: 7.3 g; Protein: 24.6 g; Cholesterol: 55 mg; Sodium: 2808 mg

Hot & Sweet Strawberry Soup

Yield: 1 Serving
Total Time: 10 Minutes
Prep Time: 5 Minutes
Cook Time: 5 Minutes

Ingredients

- 7 strawberries
- 2 tablespoons fresh lemon juice
- ¼ cup water
- Dash of cinnamon
- Vanilla liquid stevia

Directions:

In a blender, combine milk, water, lemon juice, spices and strawberries and blend until smooth; transfer to a saucepan and heat for about 3-5 minutes. Serve hot or cold garnished with mint.

Phase 3 modifications: Omit lemon juice and add three tablespoons of cream, half and half or cream cheese and serve sprinkled with phase 3 chocolate shavings or chopped roasted nuts.

Nutritional Information per Serving:

Calories: 31; Total Fat: 0.5 g; Carbs: 6.4 g; Dietary Fiber: 1.7 g; Sugars: 4.2 g; Protein: 0.7 g; Cholesterol: 0 mg; Sodium: 9 mg

Hot & Sour Thai-Style Shrimp Soup

Yield: 1 Serving
Total Time: 33 Minutes
Prep Time: 10 Minutes
Cook Time: 23 Minutes

Ingredients

- 100 grams shrimp
- 1 tablespoon chopped green onion
- 2-3 slices of fresh ginger
- 1 lemon grass stalk
- Juice of ½ lemon with rind
- 2 cups vegetable broth
- 1 tablespoon chopped cilantro
- Pinch of red pepper flakes
- Pinch of salt & pepper

Directions:

Add broth to a saucepan and bring to a rolling boil; stir in onion, lemon juice, lemongrass, ginger and pepper and simmer for about 10-15 minutes. Stir in shrimp and cilantro and continue cooking for 8 minutes more. Remove lemongrass and serve hot.

Phase 3 modifications: Add fish paste and straw mushrooms, and chili oil or hot chili paste.

Nutritional Information per Serving:

Calories: 198; Total Fat: 4.5 g; Carbs: 3.9 g; Dietary Fiber: 0.2 g; Sugars: 1.5 g; Protein: 32.6 g; Cholesterol: 211 mg; Sodium: 1772 mg

French-Style Oniony Soup

Yield: 1 Serving
Total Time: 35 Minutes
Prep Time: 10 Minutes
Cook Time: 25 Minutes

Ingredients

- 1 clove garlic, minced
- 1 onion, thinly sliced
- 2 tablespoons fresh lemon juice
- ½ teaspoon Worcestershire sauce
- 1/2 cup water
- 1 ½ cups vegetable broth
- Pinch of salt & pepper

Directions:

Add a tablespoon of lemon juice and water to a saucepan; add garlic and sauté. Transfer to a medium pot and add the remaining ingredients. Bring to a gentle boil and then lower heat. Simmer, covered, for about 20 minutes. Serve right away!

Variation: add beef to soup.

Nutritional Information per Serving:

Calories: 42; Total Fat: 2.1g; Carbs: 1.8 g; Dietary Fiber: 0.8 g; Sugars: 0.3 g; Protein: 0.9 g; Cholesterol: 0 mg; Sodium: 328 mg

Tasty Tomato Soup

Yield: 1 Serving
Total Time: 25 Minutes
Prep Time: 10 Minutes
Cook Time: 15 Minutes

Ingredients

- 1 cup vegetable Broth
- 1 large Tomato
- 1 clove Garlic, minced
- ¼ teaspoon Onion Powder
- ½ packet Stevia
- ½ teaspoon Basil
- Pinch of salt & pepper

Directions:

Add a tablespoon of broth to a saucepan and add garlic; sauté and set aside.

Puree tomato in a blender until smooth; add to garlic and bring to a gentle boil over medium heat. Stir in the remaining ingredients and simmer, covered, for about 10 minutes.

Nutritional Information per Serving:

Calories: 24; Total Fat: 1.7 g; Carbs: 1.9 g; Dietary Fiber: 1.1 g; Sugars: 0.1 g; Protein: 0.2g; Cholesterol: 0 mg; Sodium: 92 mg

Mexican Meatball Soup

Yield: 1 Serving
Total Time: 40 Minutes
Prep Time: 10 Minutes
Cook Time: 30 Minutes

Ingredients

Meatballs

- 100 grams lean ground beef
- 1clove garlic, minced
- ¼ red onion, minced
- ½ cup bread crumbs
- 1/8 teaspoon oregano
- Dash of garlic powder
- Dash of onion powder
- Pinch of salt & pepper
- Pinch of cayenne pepper
- Pinch of cumin

Broth

- 1 cup beef broth
- 1 clove garlic, minced
- 1 tablespoon chopped red onion
- 1 tablespoon chopped cilantro
- ½ cup chopped tomatoes
- ¼ teaspoon dried oregano
- Pinch of salt & pepper
- 1 cup water

Directions:

Make meatballs: in a bowl, mix ground beef, garlic, onion, Melba crumbs, chopped cilantro and powdered spices; form meatballs and place them to a saucepan; add beef broth, garlic, onion, and spices and bring to a gentle boil. Lower heat and simmer for about 30 minutes, adding tomato or celery during the last 10 minutes. Serve topped with oregano and chopped cilantro.

Phase 3 modifications: add a small amount of chopped carts.

Nutritional Information per Serving:

Calories: 313; Total Fat: 8.5 g; Carbs: 19.2 g; Dietary Fiber: 3.2 g; Sugars: 5.8 g; Protein: 38.7 g; Cholesterol: 89 mg; Sodium: 956 mg

Tasty Chicken Soup

Yield: 1 ½ cups
Total Time: 20 Minutes
Prep Time: 5 Minutes
Cook Time: 15 Minutes

Ingredients

- 3 ounces chicken breast, diced
- 3 celery stalks, sliced
- 1 ½ cups vegetable broth
- 1 teaspoon liquid aminos
- ½ teaspoon onion powder

Directions:

Combine all ingredients in a medium pan and bring to a gentle boil; lower heat and simmer for about 15 minutes or until chicken is cooked through. Serve.

Nutritional Information per Serving:

Calories: 232; Total Fat: 8.5 g; Carbs: 3.9 g; Dietary Fiber: 0.9 g; Sugars: 2.2 g; Protein: 32.3 g; Cholesterol: 76 mg; Sodium: 256 mg

Tasty Turkey Chili

Yield: 8 Servings

Total Time: 35 Minutes

Prep Time: 10 Minutes

Cook Time: 25 Minutes

Ingredients

- 2 pounds ground turkey
- 1 cup water
- 2 (15-ounce) cans diced tomatoes
- 2 teaspoons chili powder
- ½ teaspoon cumin
- 1 teaspoon garlic powder
- 1 teaspoon onion powder
- Toast
- Pinch of sea salt
- Pinch of pepper

Directions:

Brown turkey and add all the remaining ingredients; bring to a boil. Lower heat and simmer for about 20 minutes. Serve with Melba toast. Freeze extra chili for later use.

Variation: use ground chicken or beef in place of turkey.

Nutritional Information per Serving:

Calories: 245; Total Fat: 12.8 g; Carbs: 19.2 g; Dietary Fiber: 1.6g; Sugars: 3.1 g; Protein: 32.2 g; Cholesterol: 116 mg; Sodium: 580 mg

Mexican Chicken Soup

Yield: 1 Serving
Total Time: 35 Minutes
Prep Time: 10 Minutes
Cook Time: 25 Minutes

Ingredients

- 3 ounces boneless skinless chicken breast
- 15 ounce can diced tomatoes
- 1 cup vegetable broth
- ½ cup water
- ½ teaspoon onion powder
- ½ teaspoon garlic powder
- ½ teaspoon chopped celery tops
- dash of cumin
- dash chili powder
- 1 tablespoon cilantro

Directions:

Cook chicken and shred; mix in the remaining ingredients and bring to a boil. Lower heat and simmer for about 20 minutes.

Nutritional Information per Serving:

Calories: 302; Total Fat: 7.8 g; Carbs: 25 g; Dietary Fiber: 7.6 g; Sugars: 16 g; Protein: 33.8 g; Cholesterol: 76 mg; Sodium: 1752 mg

Chicken Tomato Soup

Yield: 1 Serving
Total Time: 5 Minutes
Prep Time: 10 Minutes
Cook Time: 25 Minutes

Ingredients

- 3 ounces boneless skinless chicken breast
- 15-ounce can diced tomatoes
- 1 cup vegetable broth
- ½ cup water
- ½ teaspoon onion powder
- ½ teaspoon garlic powder
- ½ teaspoon chopped celery tops

Directions:

Cook chicken and shred; add in the remaining ingredients and bring to a gentle boil. Lower heat and simmer for about 20 minutes.

Nutritional Information per Serving:

Calories: 300; Total Fat: 7.7 g; Carbs: 24.6 g; Dietary Fiber: 7.5 g; Sugars: 16 g; Protein: 33.7 g; Cholesterol: 76 mg; Sodium: 1747 mg

Cabbage & Chicken Soup

Yield: 3 Servings
Total Time: 30 Minutes
Prep Time: 10 Minutes
Cook Time: 20 Minutes

Ingredients

- 12 ounces boneless skinless chicken breast
- 2 cups vegetable broth
- 1 tablespoon chopped celery heart
- leaves- chopped
- 1 medium head cabbage, chopped
- 2 teaspoons fresh lemon juice
- 2 ½ teaspoon liquid aminos
- 1 teaspoon garlic powder
- 1 teaspoon onion powder
- 1 tablespoon chopped fresh cilantro

Directions:

Cook chicken and shred; add the remaining ingredients except cilantro and cook until cabbage is wilted. Remove from heat and serve sprinkled with cilantro.

Nutritional Information per Serving:

Calories: 308; Total Fat: 9.6 g; Carbs: 15.9 g; Dietary Fiber: 6.2 g; Sugars: 8.7 g; Protein: 39.4 g; Cholesterol: 101 mg; Sodium: 653 mg

Creamy Chicken Soup

Yield: 1 Serving
Total Time: 40 Minutes
Prep Time: 10 Minutes
Cook Time: 30 Minutes

Ingredients

- 3 ounces boneless skinless chicken breast, cooked
- 3 ounces coarsely chopped celery
- 3 cloves garlic
- 1 ½ cups vegetable broth
- 1 tablespoon onion, dehydrated
- ½ teaspoon parsley
- ½ teaspoon basil
- White pepper
- Sea salt

Directions:

In a food processor, combine all ingredients and process until chunky. Heat a saucepan over medium-high heat and add the mixture; bring to a boil. Lower heat and simmer, covered, for about 20-25 minutes.

Nutritional Information per Serving:

Calories: 237; Total Fat: 8.4 g; Carbs: 5.4 g; Dietary Fiber: 0.5 g; Sugars: 1.6 g; Protein: 32.6 g; Cholesterol: 76 mg; Sodium: 220 mg

Chicken Veggie Soup

Yield: 3 Servings
Total Time: 40 Minutes
Prep Time: 10 Minutes
Cook Time: 30 Minutes

Ingredients

- 6 cups vegetable broth 6 cups
- 9 ounces chopped chicken, cooked
- 3 celery stalks, chopped
- 1 sweet onion, chopped
- 1 ½ cup chopped cabbage
- 2 medium tomatoes, chopped, optional

Directions:

In a large pot, combine all ingredients, except cabbage and bring to a boil. Lower heat and simmer for about 20 minutes; add cabbage and simmer for about 10 minutes or until veggies are tender.

Nutritional Information per Serving:

Calories: 246; Total Fat: 5.6 g; Carbs: 11 g; Dietary Fiber: 2.9 g; Sugars: 6.5 g; Protein: 36 g; Cholesterol: 65 mg; Sodium: 1605 mg

Yield: 2 Servings
Total Time: 30 Minutes
Prep Time: 10 Minutes
Cook Time: 20 Minutes

Spicy Turkey Soup

Ingredients

- 6 ounces ground turkey, cooked
- 2 (15-ounce) can crushed or skewed tomatoes
- 3 cloves garlic, crushed
- 2 teaspoons red wine vinegar
- Pinch of parsley
- Pinch of cumin
- Pinch of basil
- Pinch of rosemary
- Pinch of red pepper flakes

Directions:

In a medium pot, combine vinegar, tomatoes, and seasonings; cook over medium heat for about 5 minutes. Stir in ground turkey and bring the mixture to a gentle boil. Lower heat and simmer for about 10 minutes. Serve warm.

Nutritional Information per Serving:

Calories: 251; Total Fat: 10.3 g; Carbs: 18.3 g; Dietary Fiber: 5.3 g; Sugars: 11.3 g; Protein: 27.3 g; Cholesterol: 87 mg; Sodium: 113 mg

Red Onion Beef Soup

Yield: 1 Serving
Total Time: 45 Minutes
Prep Time: 10 Minutes
Cook Time: 35 Minutes

Ingredients

- 3 ounces beef chunks
- 1 red onion, thinly sliced
- 1 clove garlic, minced
- ½ teaspoon Worcestershire sauce
- ½ cup water
- 1 ½ cups vegetable broth
- Sea Salt
- Pepper
- Juice of 1/2 lemon

Directions:

In a saucepan, brown beef. Add a tablespoon of lemon juice and water to another pan and sauté garlic and onion; transfer to a medium pot and add in the remaining ingredients including beef. Bring to a gentle boil; lower heat and simmer, covered, for about 20 minutes. Serve right away!

Nutritional Information per Serving:

Calories: 267; Total Fat: 7.5 g; Carbs: 8 g; Dietary Fiber: 2.5 g; Sugars: 6.2 g; Protein: 34.6 g; Cholesterol: 76 mg; Sodium: 1237 mg

Yield: 4 Servings
Total Time: 35 Minutes
Prep Time: 10 Minutes
Cook Time: 25 Minutes

Tasty Ground Beef Stew

Ingredients

- 12 ounces lean ground beef
- 2 (15-ounce) cans stewed tomatoes
- 3-4 cloves garlic, crushed
- parsley
- pinch of cumin
- basil
- pinch of rosemary
- Pinch of salt & pepper
- Pinch of red pepper flakes

Directions:

Brown the meat and drain. Rinse under warm water and return to pan. Stir in spices and tomatoes; simmer for about 10 minutes.

Variation: use chicken instead of beef.

Nutritional Information per Serving:

Calories: 200; Total Fat: 5.7 g; Carbs: 9 g; Dietary Fiber: 2.6 g; Sugars: 5.6 g; Protein: 27.8 g; Cholesterol: 76 mg; Sodium: 67 mg

HCG Poultry Entrees

Hot Chicken Curry

Yield: 1 Serving
Total Time: 35 Minutes
Prep Time: 10 Minutes
Cook Time: 25 Minutes

Ingredients

- 100 grams diced chicken
- 1 tablespoon minced onion
- ¼ cup chicken broth
- ¼ teaspoon curry powder
- Dash of onion powder
- Dash of garlic powder
- Pinch of cayenne
- Pinch of turmeric
- Pinch of salt & pepper
- Pinch of stevia

Directions:

In a small saucepan, stir spices in chicken broth until dissolved; stir in chicken, garlic, onion, and stevia and cook until chicken is cooked through and liquid is reduced by half. Serve hot.

Nutritional Information per Serving:

Calories: 170; Total Fat: 3.5 g; Carbs: 2.3 g; Dietary Fiber: 0.6 g; Sugars: 0.8 g; Protein: 30.5 g; Cholesterol: 77 mg; Sodium: 255 mg

Tasty Chicken Pesto

Yield: 1 Serving
Total Time: 25 Minutes
Prep Time: 10 Minutes
Cook Time: 15 Minutes

Ingredients

- 100 grams chicken breast, thinly sliced
- 3 tablespoons fresh lemon juice
- Pinch of salt & pepper

Pesto

- 2 tablespoons fresh lemon juice
- ¼ cup chicken broth
- 2 tablespoons apple cider vinegar
- 3 cloves raw garlic
- ¼ teaspoon dried oregano
- ¼ cup fresh basil leaves
- Pinch of salt & black pepper

Directions:

In a small bowl, mix fresh lemon, salt and pepper; add chicken and marinate for a few hours before cooking.

Add chicken to a frying pan and fry until cooked through and browned.

Make pesto: in a food processor, puree together lemon juice, chicken broth, garlic and basil; pour into chicken along with a splash of water and cook for a few minutes. Season with salt and pepper and serve right away.

Phase 3 modifications: add ¼ cup of olive oil and ¼ cup parmesan cheese to the food processor or ¼ cup walnuts or pine nuts; for a creamy pesto, add half and half and omit lemon juice.

Nutritional Information per Serving:

Calories: 165; Total Fat: 3.6 g; Carbs: 5.6 g; Dietary Fiber: 0.8 g; Sugars: 2 g; Protein: 3.8 g; Cholesterol: 64 mg; Sodium: 260 mg

Gingery Chicken

Yield: 1 Serving
Total Time: 40 Minutes
Prep Time: 10 Minutes
Cook Time: 30 Minutes

Ingredients

- 100 grams chicken
- 1 tablespoon chopped red onion
- ½ teaspoon fresh ginger
- ¼ cup chicken broth
- 4 tablespoons fresh lemon juice
- 4 tablespoons Bragg's liquid aminos
- ¼ teaspoon lemon
- Pinch of cayenne pepper
- Pinch of salt and pepper
- Pinch of stevia

Directions:

Add a splash of lemon juice and water to a small saucepan and sauté chicken until browned; stir in stevia, lemon juice, ginger, spices and salt and Bragg's and cook until chicken is cooked through, adding water periodically to deglaze the pan. Serve hot garnished with orange or lemon slices.

Nutritional Information per Serving:

Calories: 184; Total Fat: 4 g; Carbs: 3.4 g; Dietary Fiber: 0.7 g; Sugars:8 g; Protein: 30.9 g; Cholesterol: 77 mg; Sodium: 267 mg

Grilled Chicken & Green Onion

Yield: 1 Serving
Total Time: 15 Minutes
Prep Time: 10 Minutes
Cook Time: 5 Minutes

Ingredients

- 3 ounces chicken breast
- 1 green onion, chopped
- Pinch of garlic powder
- Pinch of sea salt
- Pinch of pepper

Directions:

Place chicken on grill and top with onion slices; sprinkle with garlic powder, salt and pepper and grill for about 5 minutes or until chicken is cooked through.

Variation: use fish filet instead of chicken.

Nutritional Information per Serving:

Calories: 176; Total Fat: 6.3 g; Carbs: 3.4 g; Dietary Fiber: 0.8 g; Sugars: 1.5 g; Protein: 5 g; Cholesterol: 76 mg; Sodium: 61 mg

Healthy Chicken Burgers

Yield: 2 Servings
Total Time: 20 Minutes
Prep Time: 15 Minutes
Cook Time: 5 Minutes

Ingredients

- 6 ounces ground chicken or turkey
- 1 sweet onion
- 1 tomato, thickly sliced
- 4 lettuce leaves

Directions:

Form the ground chicken into two patties and top each with onions and tomatoes; grill for about 5 minutes and sandwich each patty, with tomatoes and onions, between two lettuce leaves.

Variation: use ground beef instead of chicken.

Nutritional Information per Serving:

Calories: 191; Total Fat: 6.4 g; Carbs: 6.7 g; Dietary Fiber: 1.6 g; Sugars: 3.3 g; Protein: 5.5 g; Cholesterol: 76 mg; Sodium: 77 mg

Spicy Cucumber Chicken

Yield: 2 Servings
Total Time: 25 Minutes
Prep Time: 10 Minutes
Cook Time: 15 Minutes

Ingredients

- 6 ounces boneless skinless chicken breast
- 2 cups sliced cucumbers
- ½ teaspoon Tony Chachere's Creole Seasoning

Directions:

Cook chicken and dice into ½-inch cubes; mix with remaining ingredients and serve.

Nutritional Information per Serving:

Calories: 177; Total Fat: 6.4 g; Carbs: 3.8 g; Dietary Fiber: 0.5 g; Sugars: 1.7 g; Protein: 25.3 g; Cholesterol: 76 mg; Sodium: 75 mg

Delicious Herb Breaded Chicken

Yield: 2 Servings
Total Time: 15 Minutes
Prep Time: 10 Minutes
Cook Time: 5 Minutes

Ingredients

- 6 ounces boneless skinless chicken breast
- 4 tablespoons fresh lemon juice
- 2 melba toast, crushed
- 1/8 teaspoon oregano
- 1/8 teaspoon sea salt
- ½ teaspoon parsley flakes

Directions:

In a shallow dish, mix crushed Melba toast with spices; set aside.

Drizzle fresh lemon juice over chicken and coat with seasoned mixture; grill for about 5 minutes.

Variation: use tilapia instead of chicken.

Nutritional Information per Serving:

Calories: 173; Total Fat: 3.3 g; Carbs: 9.6 g; Dietary Fiber: 2.5 g; Sugars: 6.2 g; Protein: 8.2 g; Cholesterol: 54 mg; Sodium: 165 mg

Healthy Chicken Egg Roll

Yield: 2 Servings
Total Time: 20 Minutes
Prep Time: 10 Minutes
Cook Time: 10 Minutes

Ingredients

- 6 ounces boneless skinless grilled chicken breast, diced into ¼-inch cubes
- 3 cabbage Leaves
- 1 cup shredded cabbage
- ½ packet stevia
- 2 rounds Melba toast, crushed
- Dash sea salt
- Dash onion powder
- Dash garlic powder
- Dash Chinese 5 Spice

Directions:

Mix chicken with stevia and spices and set aside. Steam shredded cabbage for about 5 minutes; steam cabbage leaves for about 5 minutes. Drain and transfer shredded cabbage to a large bowl; mix in chicken mixture and place in cabbage leaves; top with crushed toast and wrap. Serve.

Nutritional Information per Serving:

Calories: 245; Total Fat: 4.4 g; Carbs: 11.2 g; Dietary Fiber: 4.9 g; Sugars: 6.1 g; Protein: 37.6 g; Cholesterol: 109 mg; Sodium: 342 mg

Cajun Chicken

Yield: 2 Servings
Total Time: 15 Minutes
Prep Time: 10 Minutes
Cook Time: 5 Minutes

Ingredients

- 12 ounces boneless skinless chicken breast
- 2 teaspoons water
- 1 tablespoon cayenne pepper
- ½ teaspoon sea salt
- ¼ teaspoon pepper
- ½ teaspoon onion powder
- ½ teaspoon garlic powder

Directions:

Stir all spices into water and rub onto chicken; let marinate for at least 1 hour. Grill for about 5 minutes.

Nutritional Information per Serving:

Calories: 337; Total Fat: 13.1 g; Carbs: 2.7 g; Dietary Fiber: 0.9 g; Sugars: 0.7 g; Protein: 49.7 g; Cholesterol: 151 mg; Sodium: 616 mg

Stir-Fried Chicken

Yield: 1 Serving
Total Time: 15 Minutes
Prep Time: 10 Minutes
Cook Time: 5 Minutes

Ingredients

- 3 ounces boneless skinless chicken breast
- 1 tablespoon milk
- 1 round melba toast, crushed
- Sea salt
- Pepper

Directions:

In a small bowl, mix together seasonings with Melba toast.

Dip chicken in milk and then coat with toast mix; grill for about 5 minutes.

Variation: use fish in place of chicken.

Nutritional Information per Serving:

Calories: 169; Total Fat: 6.6 g; Carbs: 3.8 g; Dietary Fiber: 1 g; Sugars: 0.76 g; Protein: 25.1 g; Cholesterol: 77 mg; Sodium: 80 mg

Marinara Chicken

Yield: 1 Servings

Total Time: 75 Minutes

Prep Time: 10 Minutes

Cook Time: 65 Minutes

Ingredients

- 3 ounces boneless skinless chicken breast
- 1 small tomato, diced
- 2 cloves garlic
- 1 teaspoon oregano
- 1 teaspoon basil
- ½ teaspoon chili powder
- Dash garlic powder
- Dash pepper

Directions:

Preheat oven to 350°F.

Add half of diced tomatoes in a casserole dish.

Sprinkle chicken with garlic powder, salt and pepper and sear in pan for about 1-2 minutes per side; transfer to a dish with tomatoes and top with minced garlic.

Toss together the remaining ingredients in a small bowl and pour over chicken; bake, covered with aluminum foil, for about 45-60 minutes. Serve warm.

Nutritional Information per Serving:

Calories: 197; Total Fat: 6.9 g; Carbs: 7.5 g; Dietary Fiber: 2.4 g; Sugars: 2.7 g; Protein: 26.2 g; Cholesterol: 76 mg; Sodium: 92 mg

Tasty Baked Chicken

Yield: 4 Servings
Total Time: 15 Minutes
Prep Time: 10 Minutes
Cook Time: 5 Minutes

Ingredients

- 12 ounces boneless skinless chicken breast
- 1 packet stevia
- Rosemary
- Thyme
- Dash of sea salt
- Dash of pepper

Directions:

In a plastic bag, combine all ingredients; seal and shake thoroughly. Grill for about 5 minutes.

Variation: use fish filet in place of chicken.

Nutritional Information per Serving:

Calories: 162; Total Fat: 6.3 g; Carbs: 0 g; Dietary Fiber: 0 g; Sugars: 0 g; Protein: 24.6 g; Cholesterol: 76 mg; Sodium: 132 mg

Oven-Fried Chicken Tenders

Yield: 1 Serving

Total Time: 40 Minutes

Prep Time: 10 Minutes

Cook Time: 30 Minutes

Ingredients

- 3 ounces chicken tenders
- 1 grissini breadstick
- Sea salt
- Paprika
- Red pepper
- Garlic powder

Directions:

Add milk in a small bowl.

In a food processor, grind breadstick until fine.

In a separate bowl, mix seasonings with breadstick powder.

Dip chicken in milk and then coat with breadstick mixture and place it in a baking dish; bake in a 350°F oven for about 30 minutes, turning halfway through. For the last 5 minutes or cooking, broil for about 2 minutes per side or until browned.

Nutritional Information per Serving:

Calories: 223; Total Fat: 8.4 g; Carbs: 13.3 g; Dietary Fiber: 1.8 g; Sugars: 6 g; Protein: 26.5 g; Cholesterol: 76 mg; Sodium: 76 mg

Ginger & Orange Chicken

Yield: 1 Serving
Total Time: 5 Minutes
Prep Time: 10 Minutes
Cook Time: 25 Minutes

Ingredients

- 3 ounces boneless skinless chicken breast, diced
- 2-3 cloves garlic, minced
- Juice of 1 orange
- Sections of 1 orange
- 1 tablespoon fresh ginger root
- ½ teaspoon basil
- Fresh lemon juice of ½ lemon
- Pepper

Directions:

Heat pan over medium heat.

Season chicken with pepper and stir fry in the pan for about 5 minutes or until browned; add garlic and continue cooking for 1 minute. Stir in lemon juice, orange juice, orange sections and basil and simmer for about 10-15 minutes.

Nutritional Information per Serving:

Calories: 175; Total Fat: 6.4 g; Carbs: 2.7 g; Dietary Fiber: 0.2 g; Sugars: 0.26 g; Protein: 25.1 g; Cholesterol: 76 mg; Sodium: 75 mg

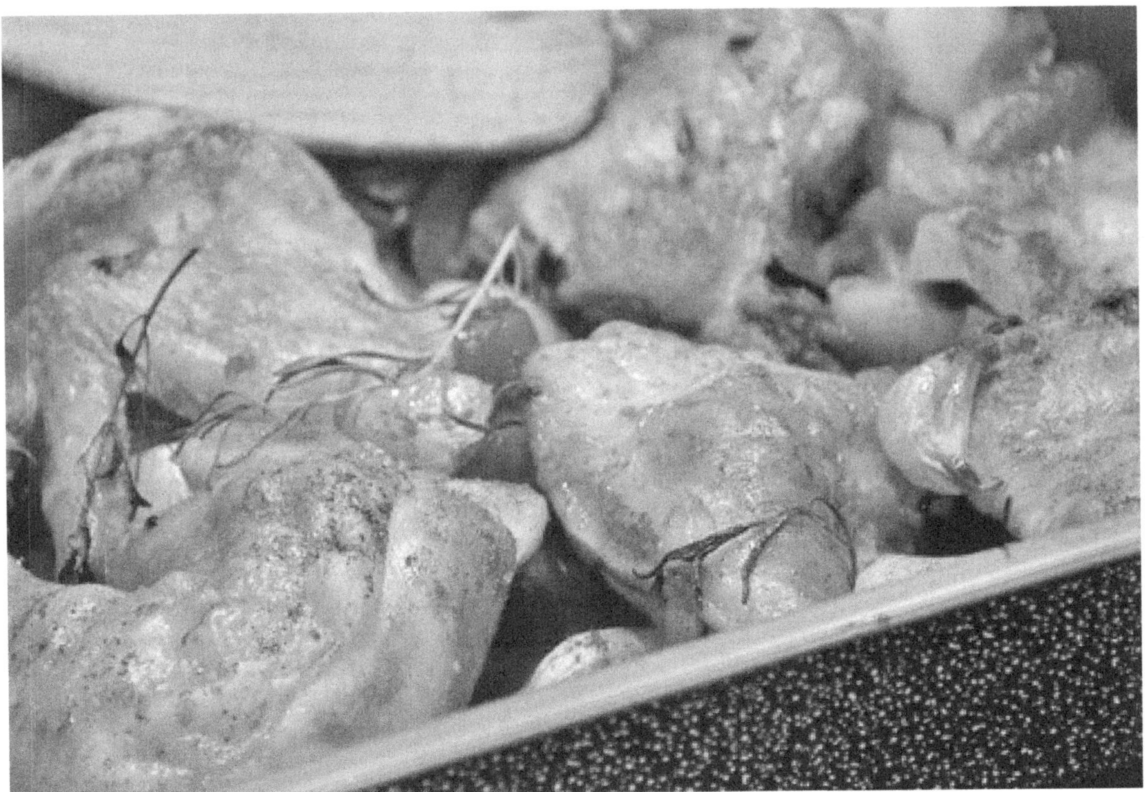

Spicy Chicken

Yield: 1 Serving

Total Time: 25 Minutes

Prep Time: 10 Minutes

Cook Time: 15 Minutes

Ingredients

- 3 ounces boneless skinless chicken breast, diced
- 5 tablespoons vegetable broth
- 3 ounces shredded cabbage
- 1 clove garlic, minced
- ½ packet stevia
- Dash of onion powder
- Dash of Chinese 5 Spice
- Dash of sea salt
- Dash of pepper

Directions:

Add a tablespoon of broth to a saucepan and sauté garlic; stir in 2 tablespoons of broth and cabbage and cook for a few minutes. Transfer cabbage to a bowl while still crunchy. Stir remaining ingredients into the pan and stir fry; return cabbage and cook for about 1-2 minutes.

Variations: use shrimp or beef instead of chicken.

Nutritional Information per Serving:

Calories: 201; Total Fat: 6.8 g; Carbs: 6.5 g; Dietary Fiber: 2.2 g; Sugars: 3.1 g; Protein: 27.4 g; Cholesterol: 76 mg; Sodium: 562 mg

Chicken Kabobs

Yield: 1 Serving
Total Time: 5 Minutes
Prep Time: 10 Minutes
Cook Time: 5 Minutes

Ingredients

- 3 ounces boneless skinless chicken breast, diced into 1-inch cubes
- 1 sweet onion, cut into wedges
- 1 teaspoon Chinese seasoning
- 2 skewers

Directions:

In a bowl, combine meat, onion and seasonings and marinate for about 4 hours; alternatively, place meat and onion on skewers and grill for about 5 minutes.

Variation: use beef in place of chicken.

Nutritional Information per Serving:

Calories: 206; Total Fat: 6.4 g; Carbs: 10.3 g; Dietary Fiber: 2.4 g; Sugars: 4.7 g; Protein: 25.8 g; Cholesterol: 76 mg; Sodium: 78 mg

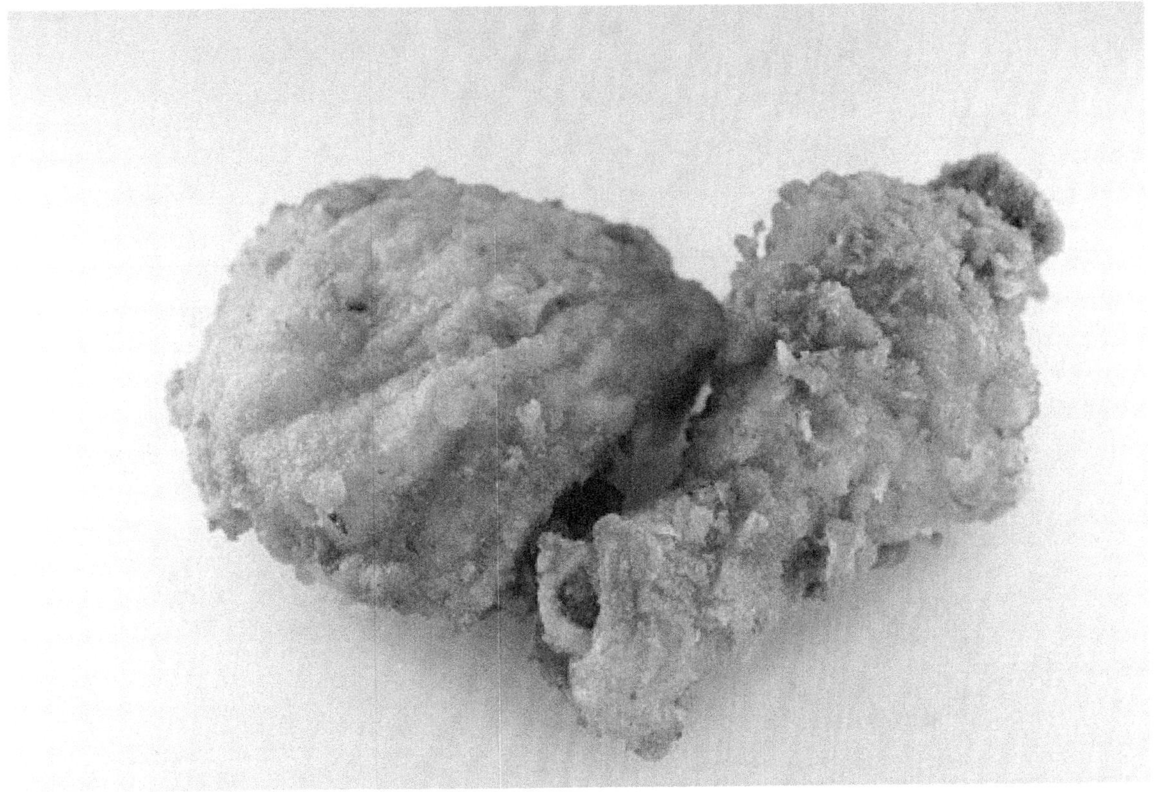

Yield: 2 Servings
Total Time: 15 Minutes
Prep Time: 10 Minutes
Cook Time: 5 Minutes

Lemony Breaded Chicken

Ingredients

- 6 ounces boneless skinless chicken breast
- fresh juice of 1 lemon
- 2 round melba toast, crushed
- sea salt
- pepper
- onion powder

Directions:

In a small bowl, mix onion powder, crushed toast, salt and pepper. Drizzle chicken with lemon juice and coat with toast mix; grill for about 5 minutes.

Variation: use 8 ounce tilapia instead of chicken.

Nutritional Information per Serving:

Calories: 238; Total Fat: 7.3 g; Carbs: 2.8 g; Dietary Fiber: 2.3 g; Sugars: 1.4 g; Protein: 28.7 g; Cholesterol: 76 mg; Sodium: 219 mg

Chicken Gumbo

Yield: 1 Serving
Total Time: 35 Minutes
Prep Time: 10 Minutes
Cook Time: 25 Minutes

Ingredients

- 3 ounces boneless skinless chicken breast, diced into 1-inch cubes
- 1 clove garlic, chopped
- 2 Roma tomatoes, chopped
- ¼ teaspoon onion powder
- ¼ teaspoon tony Chachere's creole seasoning
- garlic powder
- celery salt
- cayenne pepper
- 1 packet stevia

Directions:

Sauté chicken in a pan set over medium heat until browned; stir in remaining ingredients and simmer for about 15 minutes.

Variation: replace chicken with a variety of seafood.

Nutritional Information per Serving:

Calories: 212; Total Fat: 6.8 g; Carbs: 11 g; Dietary Fiber: 3 g; Sugars: 6.7 g; Protein: 27 g; Cholesterol: 76 mg; Sodium: 86 mg

Chili Chicken Lettuce Wraps

Yield: 4 Servings
Total Time: 35 Minutes
Prep Time: 10 Minutes
Cook Time: 25 Minutes

Ingredients

- 1 pound ground chicken or turkey
- 1 ½ cups water
- 3 cups chopped tomatoes
- ½ cup chopped onion
- 1 teaspoon garlic powder
- 1 teaspoon chili powder
- ½ teaspoon oregano
- Cayenne Pepper
- Sea Salt
- Pepper
- Lettuce Leaves

Directions:

Sauté onion and meat until browned; drain and rinse; stir in remaining ingredients and simmer for about 20 minutes, except lettuce leaves. Place the mixture on lettuce leaves and roll up; serve.

Variation: use beef instead of turkey or chicken.

Nutritional Information per Serving:

Calories: 251; Total Fat: 8.8 g; Carbs: 7.6 g; Dietary Fiber: 2.3 g; Sugars: 4.4 g; Protein: 34.4 g; Cholesterol: 101 mg; Sodium: 114 mg

Spiced Basil Tomato Chicken

Yield: 1 Serving
Total Time: 25 Minutes
Prep Time: 10 Minutes
Cook Time: 15 Minutes

Ingredients

- 3 ounces boneless skinless chicken breast, diced
- 1 cup chopped fresh tomatoes
- ¼ cup water
- 2 tablespoons fresh lemon juice
- 2 tablespoons chopped onion
- 2 tablespoons minced garlic cloves
- ¼ teaspoon oregano
- ¼ teaspoon garlic powder
- ¼ teaspoon onion powder
- 3 fresh basil leaves, sliced
- sea salt
- pepper
- cayenne pepper

Directions:

Sauté chicken in lemon juice until browned; stir in oregano, onion, garlic and water; cook until chicken is cooked through. Stir in tomatoes and basil and simmer for about 10 minutes; season with salt and pepper and serve.

Nutritional Information per Serving:

Calories: 241; Total Fat: 7.1 g; Carbs: 16.4 g; Dietary Fiber: 3.4 g; Sugars: 6.8 g; Protein: 28 g; Cholesterol: 76 mg; Sodium: 94 mg

Yield: 1 Serving
Total Time: 10 Minutes
Prep Time: 10 Minutes
Cook Time: N/A

Chicken Strawberry Salad

Ingredients

- 3 ounces chopped lettuce
- 3 ounces shredded boneless skinless chicken breast, grilled
- 6 strawberries
- 1 tablespoon strawberry vinaigrette

Directions:

In a salad bowl, toss all ingredients together until lettuce and chicken are well coated. Serve.

Nutritional Information per Serving:

Calories: 196; Total Fat: 6.7 g; Carbs: 8.1 g; Dietary Fiber: 2 g; Sugars: 4.4 g; Protein: 25.5 g; Cholesterol: 76 mg; Sodium: 79 mg

Turkey Lettuce Wraps

Yield: 4 Servings
Total Time: 25 Minutes
Prep Time: 10 Minutes
Cook Time: 15 Minutes

Ingredients

- 1 pound ground turkey, grilled
- sea salt
- black pepper
- 1 tablespoon garlic powder
- onion powder
- ½ cup chopped sweet onion
- 1 green onion, chopped
- 1 cup diced Roma tomatoes
- several iceburg lettuce leaves

Directions:

Brown turkey, drain and rinse; stir in tomatoes, onions and spices and simmer for about 10 minutes. Place the turkey mixture on a lettuce leaf and roll up to make wraps.

Variations: sprinkle meat mixture over lettuce salad. Use beef of chicken instead of turkey.

Nutritional Information per Serving:

Calories: 243; Total Fat: 2.6 g; Carbs: 4.9 g; Dietary Fiber: 1.6 g; Sugars: 2.4 g; Protein: 32 g; Cholesterol: 116 mg; Sodium: 125 mg

Chicken Tarragon

Yield: 1 Serving
Total Time: 25 Minutes
Prep Time: 10 Minutes
Cook Time: 15 Minutes

Ingredients

- 100 grams chicken breast
- 2 tablespoons fresh lemon juice
- ¼ cup chicken broth
- 1 clove garlic minced
- 1 tablespoon chopped red onion
- ½ teaspoon chopped tarragon
- Dash of mustard powder
- ¼ cup tarragon & garlic infusion
- Pinch of salt & pepper

Directions:

In a small saucepan, heat onion, garlic, vinegar and chicken broth; add chicken and sauté for about 10 minutes or until chicken is cooked through and liquid is reduced, adding splashes of water periodically to deglaze the pan. Serve immediately.

Nutritional Information per Serving:

Calories: 142; Total Fat: 3.3 g; Carbs: 3.1 g; Dietary Fiber: 0.5 g; Sugars: 1.3 g; Protein: 23.1 g; Cholesterol: 64 mg; Sodium: 249 mg

Chicken Apple Sausage

Yield: 1 Serving
Total Time: 25 Minutes
Prep Time: 10 Minutes
Cook Time: 15 Minutes

Ingredients

- 100 grams ground chicken breast
- ½ red onion, minced
- 2 tablespoons minced apple
- 2 tablespoons fresh apple juice
- 2 tablespoons chicken broth
- ½ cup bread crumbs
- Dash of nutmeg
- Dash of cinnamon
- Dash of onion powder
- Dash of garlic powder
- Dash of stevia
- Dash of cayenne
- Dash of salt & black pepper

Directions:

In a small bowl, stir together dry spices, diced apples, and ground chicken, apple juice and minced onion until well combined; form three patties from the mixture and add to chicken broth in a saucepan. Cook until cooked through and lightly browned.

Nutritional Information per Serving:

Calories: 381; Total Fat: 2.1 g; Carbs: 70.6 g; Dietary Fiber: 11.4 g; Sugars: 53.2 g; Protein: 27.1 g; Cholesterol: 63 mg; Sodium: 152 mg

Chicken Asparagus Bake

Yield: 1 Serving
Total Time: 40 Minutes
Prep Time: 10 Minutes
Cook Time: 30 Minutes

Ingredients

- 100 grams diced chicken
- 2 tablespoons chopped red onion
- 1 clove garlic, minced
- ½ cup chopped asparagus
- ½ cup bread crumbs
- ½ cup chicken broth
- Dash of salt & pepper
- Dash of paprika

Directions:

In a small baking dish, mix asparagus, chicken, spices and liquids; bake in a 375°F oven for about 30 minutes or until hot and bubbly. Serve topped with paprika and crushed toast.

Nutritional Information per Serving:

Calories: 182; Total Fat: 3.8 g; Carbs: 3.2 g; Dietary Fiber: 0.9 g; Sugars: 1.5 g; Protein: 32 g; Cholesterol: 77 mg; Sodium: 446 mg

Sweet Lemon Chicken

Yield: 1 Serving
Total Time: 40 Minutes
Prep Time: 10 Minutes
Cook Time: 30 Minutes

Ingredients

- 100 grams sliced chicken
- ¼ cup chicken broth
- ½ lemon with rind, sliced
- 1 cup water
- 1 tablespoon Bragg's liquid aminos
- Pinch of salt
- Pinch of stevia
- Dash of cayenne pepper

Directions:

Add lemon slices to a pan with water and boil until pulp comes out; add chicken, broth, spices and Bragg's and simmer for a few minutes until chicken is cooked through and the sauce is reduced by half.

Serve garnished with mint, lemon zest or lemon slices.

Nutritional Information per Serving:

Calories: 161; Total Fat: 3.4 g; Carbs: 0.4 g; Dietary Fiber: 0.1 g; Sugars: 0.2g; Protein: 30.2 g; Cholesterol: 76 mg; Sodium: 94 mg

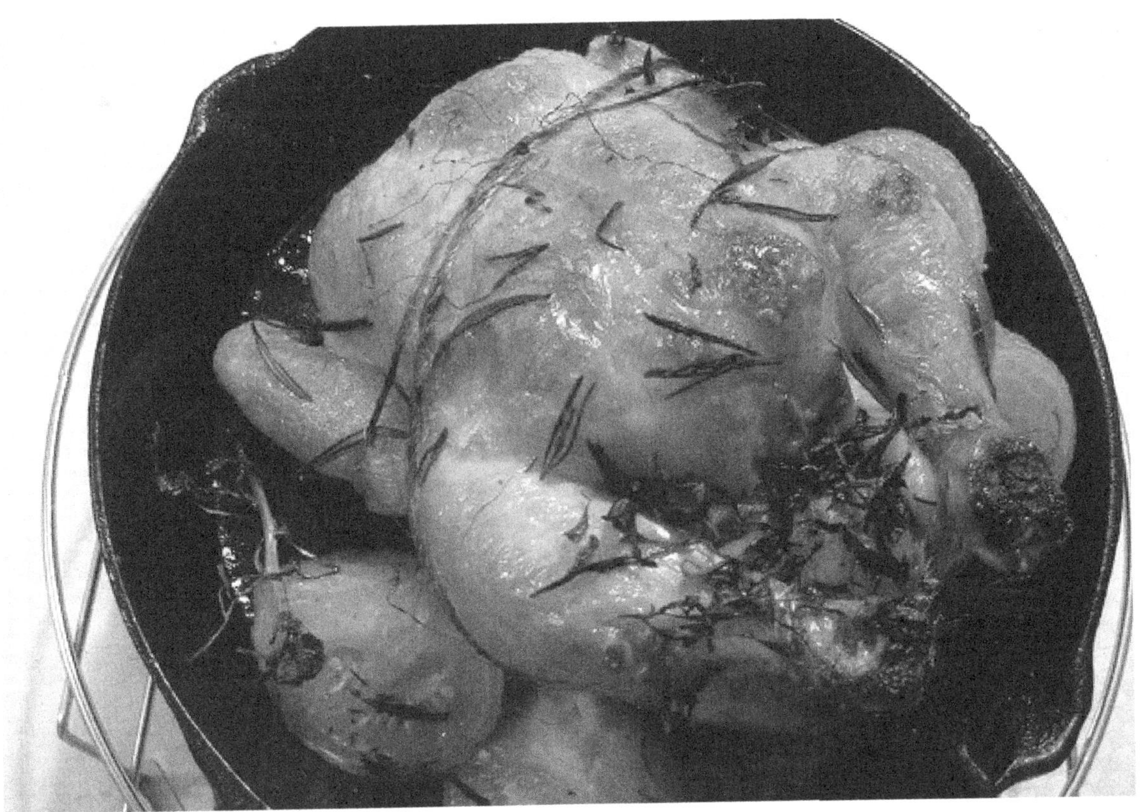

Yield: 1 Serving
Total Time: 30 Minutes
Prep Time: 10 Minutes
Cook Time: 20 Minutes

Rosemary Chicken

Ingredients

- 100 grams chicken breast, diced
- 3 tablespoons fresh lemon juice
- ¼ cup chicken broth
- ½ cup bread crumbs
- ¼ teaspoon garlic powder
- ¼ teaspoon onion powder
- ½ teaspoon fresh rosemary
- Pinch of lemon zest
- Pinch of Salt & pepper

Directions:

Mix lemon juice, rosemary and salt; add chicken and marinate for a few hours.

In a shallow bowl, mix Melba crumbs and spices and coat chicken with the mixture. Place chicken in a baking dish and add broth; top with more spices and bake in a 350°F oven for about 20 minutes or until chicken is cooked through.

Remove from oven and drizzle the chicken with fresh lemon juice and sprinkle with salt and pepper. Serve garnished with lemon slices and chopped parsley.

Nutritional Information per Serving:

Calories: 331; Total Fat: 16.3 g; Carbs: 25.7 g; Dietary Fiber: 3.6 g; Sugars: 16.5 g; Protein: 26 g; Cholesterol: 64 mg; Sodium: 327 mg

Chicken Tacos

Yield: 1 Serving
Total Time: 35 Minutes
Prep Time: 10 Minutes
Cook Time: 25 Minutes

Ingredients

- 100 grams ground chicken breast
- 2 large lettuce leaves
- 1 tablespoon chopped onion
- 1 clove garlic, minced
- ¼ cup chicken broth
- 1 tablespoon chopped cilantro
- Pinch of cumin
- Pinch of cayenne pepper
- 1/8 teaspoon oregano

Directions:

Cook chicken in broth in a small pan; stir in spices, garlic and onion and continue cooking for a few minutes. Serve the chicken taco style in romaine leaves or butter lettuce or serve topped with salsa.

Nutritional Information per Serving:

Calories: 123; Total Fat: 1.4 g; Carbs: 1.54 g; Dietary Fiber: 0.4 g; Sugars: 0. 6 g; Protein: 26.4 g; Cholesterol: 63 mg; Sodium: 241 mg

Herbed Tomato Chicken

Yield: 1 Serving
Total Time: 25 Minutes
Prep Time: 10 Minutes
Cook Time: 15 Minutes

Ingredients

- 100 grams cubed chicken
- 2 cloves garlic, sliced
- 2 tablespoons chopped red onion
- 1 cup chopped tomato
- 2 tablespoons fresh lemon juice
- ¼ cup chicken broth
- 3 leaves basil, chopped
- 1/8 teaspoon oregano
- Pinch of cayenne
- Dash of onion powder
- Dash of garlic powder
- Pinch of salt & pepper

Directions:

In a small saucepan, add lemon juice and sauté chicken until browned; stir in spices, onion, garlic and water and cook until chicken is cooked through. Stir in basil and fresh tomatoes and cook for about 5-10 minutes. Season with salt and pepper and serve garnished with fresh basil.

Nutritional Information per Serving:

Calories: 212; Total Fat: 4 g; Carbs: 10.4 g; Dietary Fiber: 2.9 g; Sugars: 6.6 g; Protein: 32.4 g; Cholesterol: 77 mg; Sodium: 290 mg

Sweet Mustard Chicken

Yield: 1 Serving
Total Time: 20 Minutes
Prep Time: 10 Minutes
Cook Time: 10 Minutes

Ingredients

- 100 grams chicken breast
- 1 tablespoon chopped red onion
- 2 tablespoons Bragg's liquid aminos
- ¼ cup chicken broth
- ½ teaspoon garlic powder
- ¼ teaspoon ginger powder
- 1/8 teaspoon mustard powder
- Pinch of salt & pepper
- Pinch of stevia

Directions:

In a small saucepan, stir spices in chicken broth and add chicken, and onion; cook over medium heat for about 5-10 minutes or until chicken is cooked through.

Nutritional Information per Serving:

Calories: 136; Total Fat: 3 g; Carbs: 2.7 g; Dietary Fiber: 0.5 g; Sugars: 1 g; Protein: 22.9 g; Cholesterol: 64 mg; Sodium: 243 mg

Chicken Cacciatore

Yield: 1 Serving
Total Time: 35 Minutes
Prep Time: 10 Minutes
Cook Time: 25 Minutes

Ingredients

- 100 grams chicken breast, diced
- 2 cloves garlic, minced
- 2 tablespoons chopped red onion
- ¼ cup chicken broth
- 2 cups chopped tomatoes
- 2 tablespoons tomato paste
- 1 tablespoon Bragg's liquid aminos
- 2 tablespoons fresh lemon juice
- ¼ teaspoon garlic powder
- 1 tablespoon apple cider vinegar
- ¼ teaspoon onion powder
- Pinch of stevia
- Pinch of cayenne
- 1 bay leaf

Directions:

In a small saucepan, cook together chicken, onion, garlic, and lemon juice until chicken is browned; stir in chicken broth, spices, vinegar, tomato and tomato paste; simmer for about 20 minutes, stirring frequently. Discard bay leaf before serving.

Nutritional Information per Serving:

Calories: 205; Total Fat: 3.6 g; Carbs: 16.9 g; Dietary Fiber: 4.1 g; Sugars: 10.7 g; Protein: 26 g; Cholesterol: 64 mg; Sodium: 290 mg

Sweet & Sour Chicken

Yield: 1 Serving
Total Time: 40 Minutes
Prep Time: 10 Minutes
Cook Time: 30 Minutes

Ingredients

- 100 grams chicken breast
- ½ red onion, minced
- ½ orange, ½ lemon with rind
- 1 tablespoon lemon zest
- 2 tablespoons apple cider vinegar
- 1 tablespoon Bragg's liquid aminos
- 1 cup water
- 1 tablespoon hot sauce
- Dash of garlic powder
- Dash of onion powder
- Pinch of stevia
- Pinch of cayenne pepper
- Pinch of salt and pepper

Directions:

Place ½ lemon and ½ orange rinds in a small saucepan with water and bring to a boil until pulp comes off rind. Discard rinds, scraping out the remaining juice and pulp with a spoon; stir in stevia, onion and spices and add chicken. Cook until chicken is cooked through and liquid is reduced by half. Stir in garlic powder and onion powder and serve right away garnished with lemon slices.

Phase 3 modifications: add fresh amounts of chopped mushrooms, bell pepper and fresh pineapple.

Nutritional Information per Serving:

Calories: 172; Total Fat: 2.7 g; Carbs: 13 g; Dietary Fiber: 2.6 g; Sugars: 9.5 g; Protein: 22.4 g; Cholesterol: 64 mg; Sodium: 441 mg

Chicken Paprika

Yield: 1 Serving
Total Time: 30 Minutes
Prep Time: 10 Minutes
Cook Time: 20 Minutes

Ingredients

- 100 grams chicken
- 1 clove garlic, minced
- 1 tablespoon chopped red onion
- 3 tablespoons tomato paste
- ½ cup chicken broth
- 1 teaspoon paprika
- Pinch of salt & pepper
- 1 bay leaf

Directions:

In a saucepan, mix together onion, garlic, chicken, broth, spices and tomato paste; simmer for about 20 minutes and serve garnished with sliced tomato and chopped parsley.

Phase 3 modifications: Heat olive oil or butter and sauté chicken and then add ¼ cup sour cream, broth and tomato.

Nutritional Information per Serving:

Calories: 220; Total Fat: 4.2 g; Carbs: 11.7 g; Dietary Fiber: 3 g; Sugars: 6.8 g; Protein: 33.9 g; Cholesterol: 77 mg; Sodium: 493 mg

Bruchetta Chicken

Yield: 1 Serving
Total Time: 45 Minutes
Prep Time: 20 Minutes
Cook Time: 25 Minutes

Ingredients

- 100 grams chicken breast, diced
- 2 cloves garlic, chopped
- ½ cup bread crumbs
- 2 medium tomatoes
- 2 tablespoons apple cider vinegar
- 1 tablespoon Bragg's liquid aminos
- 2 tablespoons lemon juice
- Pinch of marjoram
- Pinch of dried oregano
- 3 large fresh basil, chopped
- Pinch of salt & black pepper

Directions:

Marinate chicken in vinegar, Bragg's lemon juice, salt and pepper.

In a small bowl, mix dry spices and crumbs; coat chicken with the mixture and fry in a pan until golden brown.

Make bruschetta sauce: In a small bowl, mix vinegar, lemon juice, salt, pepper, finely chopped tomatoes, and crushed basil until well combined; refrigerate until chilled.

Serve hot chicken topped with chilled bruschetta sauce.

Phase 3 modifications: Drizzle chicken with olive oil and fry; use balsamic vinegar instead of bruschetta and serve chicken topped with provolone or parmesan cheese.

Nutritional Information per Serving:

Calories: 182; Total Fat: 3.3 g; Carbs: 12.7 g; Dietary Fiber: 3.3 g; Sugars: 7.3 g; Protein: 24 g; Cholesterol: 64 mg; Sodium: 72 mg

Yield: 1 Serving
Total Time: 30 Minutes
Prep Time: 10 Minutes
Cook Time: 20 Minutes

Oregano Chicken

Ingredients

- 100 grams chicken breast
- ¼ cup chicken broth
- 1 teaspoon dried oregano
- ¼ teaspoon onion powder
- ¼ teaspoon garlic powder
- Pinch of salt & pepper
- ½ cup bread crumbs

Directions:

Mix dry spices with crumbs; dip chicken in broth and dust with Melba mix. Add t a baking dish and add the remaining broth; bake in a 350°F oven for about 15-20 minutes or until browned and crusty.

Phase 3 modifications: Dip the chicken in beaten egg and coat with Melba mix or parmesan; fry in olive oil and serve topped with lemon butter sauce and parmesan or marinara sauce and cheese.

Nutritional Information per Serving:

Calories: 133; Total Fat: 3 g; Carbs: 2.3 g; Dietary Fiber: 0.8 g; Sugars: 0.6 g; Protein: 22.8 g; Cholesterol: 64 mg; Sodium: 243 mg

Citric Moroccan Chicken

Yield: 1 Serving
Total Time: 40 Minutes
Prep Time: 10 Minutes
Cook Time: 30 Minutes

Ingredients

- 100 grams chicken breast
- ½ red onion, minced
- Juice of ½ lemon
- Pinch of lemon zest
- Pinch of saffron
- Pinch of ground coriander
- Pinch of ginger
- Pinch of salt & pepper
- Lemon slices

Directions:

Soak saffron in fresh lemon juice; crush into paste and then add dry spices. Dip in chicken and rub remaining spices into chicken; sprinkle with salt and pepper and wrap in foil; place in baking dish and cover with lemon slices and saffron mi. bake in a 350°F oven for about 20-30 minutes or until chicken is cooked through.

Nutritional Information per Serving:

Calories: 122; Total Fat: 2.6 g; Carbs: 1.9 g; Dietary Fiber: 0.5 g; Sugars: 0.6 g; Protein: 21.4 g; Cholesterol: 64 mg; Sodium: 52 mg

Barbecued Chicken

Yield: 1 Serving
Total Time: 35 Minutes
Prep Time: 10 Minutes
Cook Time: 25 Minutes

Ingredients

- 100 grams chicken breast
- 1 serving barbecue sauce

Directions:

Coat the chicken with barbecue sauce; fry in a splash of water in a frying pan over low heat until cooked through. Serve hot sprinkled with salt and pepper.

Nutritional Information per Serving:

Calories: 114; Total Fat: 2.5 g; Carbs: 1 g; Dietary Fiber: 0.4 g; Sugars: 0.6 g; Protein: 21.2 g; Cholesterol: 64 mg; Sodium: 51 mg

Buffalo Chicken Fingers

Yield: 1 Serving
Total Time: 25 Minutes
Prep Time: 10 Minutes
Cook Time: 15 Minutes

Ingredients

- 100 grams chicken, sliced into strips
- 4 tablespoons fresh lemon juice
- 2 tablespoons hot sauce
- Bread crumbs
- Pinch of salt & black pepper

Directions:

Marinate chicken in fresh lemon juice and salt for a few hours and then coat with crushed crumbs; fry in a pan until cooked through and browned. Toss with black pepper and hot sauce and serve with raw celery, garnished with parsley.

Nutritional Information per Serving:

Calories: 169; Total Fat: 3.6 g; Carbs: 1.8 g; Dietary Fiber: 0.4 g; Sugars: 1.6 g; Protein: 29.6g; Cholesterol: 77 mg; Sodium: 869 mg

Baked Apple Chicken

Yield: 1 Serving
Total Time: 35 Minutes
Prep Time: 10 Minutes
Cook Time: 25 Minutes

Ingredients

- 100 grams diced chicken
- 1 tablespoon apple cider vinegar
- 2 tablespoons fresh lemon juice
- ½ apple, chopped
- 1/8 teaspoon cinnamon
- Pinch of cayenne
- Pinch of stevia
- Pinch of salt & pepper

Directions:

Brown chicken in a splash of lemon juice; stir in apple, lemon juice, vinegar, cayenne, cinnamon, stevia, and salt. Transfer to a baking dish and add lemon juice and vinegar; bake in a 350°F oven for about 20 minutes. Serve with more apple slices on side.

Nutritional Information per Serving:

Calories: 221; Total Fat: 3.5 g; Carbs: 16.6 g; Dietary Fiber: 3.1 g; Sugars: 12.3 g; Protein: 29.6 g; Cholesterol: 77 mg; Sodium: 71 mg

Orange Glazed Chicken Breast

Yield: 1 Serving
Total Time: 30 Minutes
Prep Time: 10 Minutes
Cook Time: 20 Minutes

Ingredients

- 100 grams chicken
- 1 serving sweet orange marinade or spicy orange sauce

Directions:

Cook chicken in orange sauce in a pan for about 20 minutes or until chicken is cooked through.

Nutritional Information per Serving:

Calories: 118; Total Fat: 4.1 g; Carbs: 7.2 g; Dietary Fiber: 1.4 g; Sugars: 3.6 g; Protein: 21.2 g; Cholesterol: 64 mg; Sodium: 71 mg

Garlicky Roasted Chicken

Yield: 1 Serving
Total Time: 30 Minutes
Prep Time: 10 Minutes
Cook Time: 20 Minutes

Ingredients

- 100 grams chicken, diced
- 2 cloves garlic, chopped
- ½ cup bread crumbs
- 1 tablespoon Bragg's liquid aminos
- 2 tablespoons fresh lemon juice
- ¼ cup chicken broth
- ½ teaspoon garlic powder
- ¼ teaspoon onion powder
- Pinch of salt & pepper

Directions:

Marinate chicken in wet ingredients; mix Melba crumbs with dry spices and rub into chicken. Place chicken in a baking dish and add in the marinade; top with garlic slices and bake in a 375°F oven for about 20 minutes or until chicken is cooked through. Serve garnished with parsley.

Phase 3 modifications: Drizzle chicken with olive oil before cooking and top with parmesan and bake.

Nutritional Information per Serving:

Calories: 282; Total Fat: 5.1 g; Carbs: 21.9 g; Dietary Fiber: 1.5 g; Sugars: 3 g; Protein: 34.3 g; Cholesterol: 77 mg; Sodium: 458 mg

Savory Baked Chicken

Yield: 1 Serving
Total Time: 30 Minutes
Prep Time: 10 Minutes
Cook Time: 20 Minutes

Ingredients

- 100 grams chicken breast
- ½ cup bread crumbs
- 1 tablespoon Bragg's liquid aminos
- 2 tablespoons fresh lemon juice
- ½ cup chicken broth
- 1 teaspoon chopped parsley
- Pinch of dried rosemary
- 1/8 teaspoon thyme
- ¼ teaspoon garlic powder
- ¼ teaspoon onion powder
- Pinch of salt & pepper

Directions:

Mix dried spices and Melba powder; dip chicken in Bragg's and lemon juice and coat with the herb mixture. Bake in a 350°F oven for about 20 minutes or until chicken is cooked through.

Phase 3 modifications: add parmesan to spice mix and dip chicken in egg before coating; drizzle with olive oil.

Nutritional Information per Serving:

Calories: 147; Total Fat: 3.5 g; Carbs: 2.6 g; Dietary Fiber: 0.4 g; Sugars: 1.4 g; Protein: 24.1 g; Cholesterol: 64 mg; Sodium: 442 mg

Mexican Cilantro Chicken

Yield: 1 Serving
Total Time: 35 Minutes
Prep Time: 10 Minutes
Cook Time: 25 Minutes

Ingredients

- 100 grams chicken, diced
- 1 tablespoon chopped red onion
- ¼ clove garlic, minced
- Chopped tomatoes
- 2 tablespoons fresh lemon juice
- ½ cup chicken broth
- Fresh chopped cilantro
- Pinch of cumin
- Pinch of cayenne
- ¼ teaspoon dried oregano
- ¼ teaspoon chili powder
- Pinch of salt & pepper

Directions:

Brown chicken in a splash of lemon juice; stir in chicken broth, more lemon juice and spices and cook until chicken is cooked through; stir in cilantro and tomatoes and continue cooking for 5-10 minutes more.

Nutritional Information per Serving:

Calories: 210; Total Fat: 4.5 g; Carbs: 8 g; Dietary Fiber: 2.3 g; Sugars: 4.8 g; Protein: 33.1 g; Cholesterol: 77 mg; Sodium: 654 mg

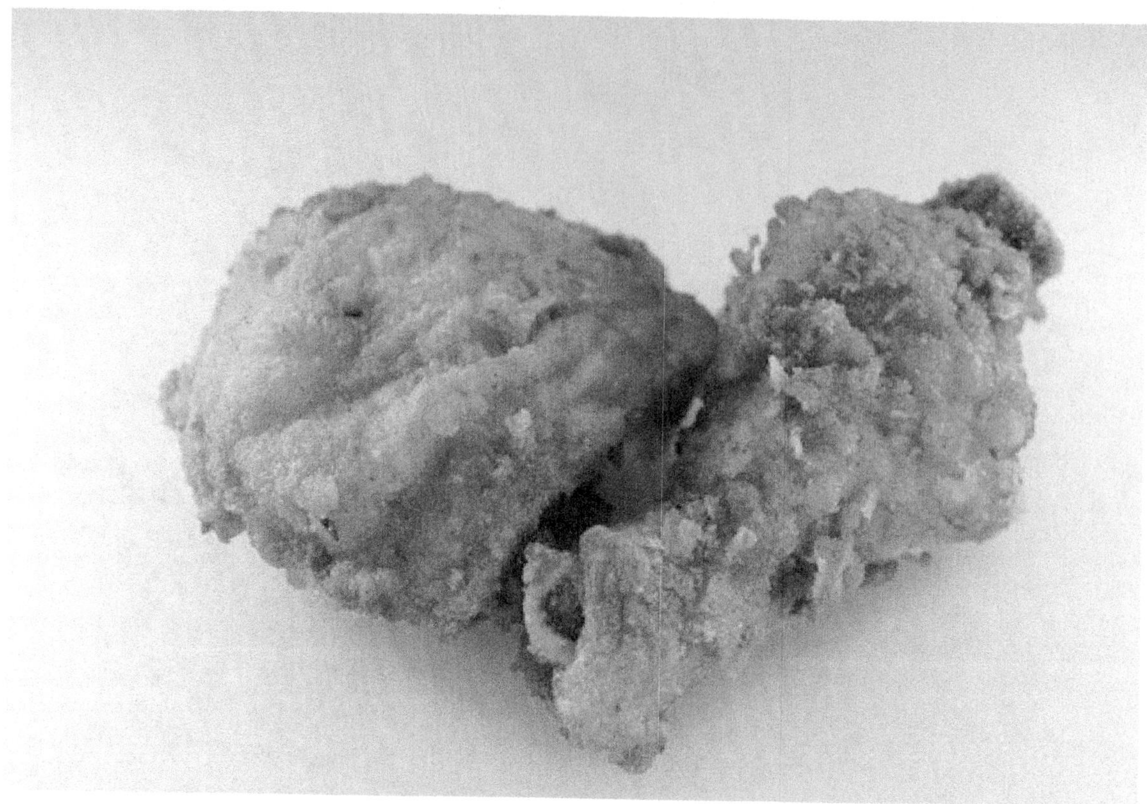

Spiced Chicken Patties

Yield: 1 Serving
Total Time: 40 Minutes
Prep Time: 10 Minutes
Cook Time: 30 Minutes

Ingredients

- 100 grams ground chicken breast
- 1 clove garlic, minced
- ½ red onion, minced
- Dash of garlic powder
- Dash of onion powder
- Pinch of cayenne pepper
- Pinch of salt & pepper

Directions:

In a small bowl, mix all ingredients until well combined; form three patties and fry in a saucepan, deglazing with water to keep chicken moist. Cook until chicken is cooked through and serve.

Nutritional Information per Serving:

Calories: 114; Total Fat: 0.9 g; Carbs: 1.6 g; Dietary Fiber: 0.4 g; Sugars: 0.6 g; Protein: 25.2 g; Cholesterol: 63 mg; Sodium: 50 mg

Middle Eastern Spicy Chicken

Yield: 1 Serving
Total Time: 40 Minutes
Prep Time: 10 Minutes
Cook Time: 30 Minutes

Ingredients

- 100 grams chicken
- 1/8 teaspoon grated ginger
- 1 clove garlic, minced
- ½ red onion, minced
- 1 cup chopped fresh tomatoes
- 3 tablespoons fresh lemon juice
- ½ cup chicken broth
- Dash of cinnamon
- Dash of cumin
- ¼ teaspoon allspice
- Pinch of salt & pepper

Directions:

Dissolve spices in liquid ingredients in a saucepan and bring to a gentle boil; stir in chicken and tomatoes and simmer for about 20-30 minutes.

Nutritional Information per Serving:

Calories: 222; Total Fat: 4.6 g; Carbs: 10.3 g; Dietary Fiber: 2.9 g; Sugars: 6.5 g; Protein: 33.6 g; Cholesterol: 77 mg; Sodium: 464 mg

Szechwan Chicken with Cabbage

Yield: 1 Serving
Total Time: 25 Minutes
Prep Time: 10 Minutes
Cook Time: 15 Minutes

Ingredients

- 100 grams chicken breast
- 1 cup chopped cabbage
- 1 tablespoon chopped green onion
- 1 clove garlic, minced
- 1 teaspoon hot sauce
- 3 tablespoons Bragg's liquid aminos
- 1 cup chicken broth
- Pinch of powdered ginger
- Pinch of red pepper flakes
- Pinch of stevia

Directions:

Brown chicken in a splash of water and Bragg's; stir in spices and broth and simmer for about 5 minutes. Stir in cabbage and continue cooking for 10 minutes or until cabbage is tender. Serve topped with green onions and drizzled with more Bragg's and lemon juice.

Nutritional Information per Serving:

Calories: 179; Total Fat: 4.1 g; Carbs: 6.9 g; Dietary Fiber: 2.5 g; Sugars: 3.8 g; Protein: 27.4 g; Cholesterol: 64 mg; Sodium: 958 mg

Slow Cooker Chicken

Yield: 1 Serving

Total Time: 3 Hours 10 Minutes

Prep Time: 10 Minutes

Cook Time: 3 Hours

Ingredients

- 100 gram chicken breast
- 5 cloves chopped garlic
- ½ cup chopped red onion
- 1 teaspoon whole black peppercorns
- ½ teaspoon thyme
- 1 teaspoon onion powder
- ½ teaspoon cayenne
- 1 teaspoon paprika
- 1 teaspoon garlic powder
- Pinch of salt & pepper

Directions:

Add chicken to a crockpot and cover with water; stir in onion and spices and cook on medium heat for about 3 hours.

Variations: Add fresh chopped tomatoes or a can of tomato paste. For a richer flavor, add poultry mix spice.

Nutritional Information per Serving:

Calories: 193; Total Fat: 3.2 g; Carbs: 17.7 g; Dietary Fiber: 3.8 g; Sugars: 4.5 g; Protein: 24.2 g; Cholesterol: 64 mg; Sodium: 60 mg

Cinnamon Chicken

Yield: 1 Serving
Total Time: 30 Minutes
Prep Time: 10 Minutes
Cook Time: 20 Minutes

Ingredients

- 100 grams of chicken
- ½ cup chicken broth
- ½ cup bread crumbs
- Dash of garlic powder
- 1/8 teaspoon curry powder
- Pinch of cardamom
- Pinch of nutmeg
- ¼ teaspoon ground cinnamon
- Pinch of stevia
- Pinch of salt & pepper

Directions:

In a small bowl, mix half of dry spices and Melba crumbs; dip chicken in broth and dust with spice mix. Place in a baking dish and add broth and the remaining spices; top with remaining Melba mix and bake in a 350°F oven for about 20 minutes or until chicken is cooked through.

Nutritional Information per Serving:

Calories: 176; Total Fat: 3.9 g; Carbs: 1.7 g; Dietary Fiber: 0.6 g; Sugars: 0.5 g; Protein: 31.6 g; Cholesterol: 77 mg; Sodium: 445 mg

Tangy Vinegar Chicken

Yield: 1 Serving
Total Time: 40 Minutes
Prep Time: 10 Minutes
Cook Time: 30 Minutes

Ingredients

- 100 grams chicken breast
- 1 clove garlic, chopped
- 1 tablespoon chopped red onion
- 2 tablespoons fresh lemon juice
- ¼ cup apple cider vinegar
- ¼ cup chicken broth
- Pinch of salt & pepper

Directions:

Mix garlic, onion, stock, vinegar, salt and pepper in a saucepan; add chicken and cook until chicken is cooked through, deglazing pan with splashes of water.

Nutritional Information per Serving:

Calories: 152; Total Fat: 3.1 g; Carbs: 3.4 g; Dietary Fiber: 0.4 g; Sugars: 1.5 g; Protein: 23 g; Cholesterol: 64 mg; Sodium: 252 mg

Spicy Mustard Chicken

Yield: 1 Serving
Total Time: 25 Minutes
Prep Time: 10 Minutes
Cook Time: 15 Minutes

Ingredients

- 100 grams chicken
- 2 tablespoons fresh lemon juice
- ½ cup chicken broth
- Pinch of stevia
- 1/8 teaspoon tarragon
- ¼ teaspoon dried basil
- 1 tablespoon homemade mustard
- Pinch of salt & pepper

Directions:

Mix spices, lemon juice and broth in a saucepan; add chicken and cook for about 10 minutes or until cooked through, deglazing pan with splashes of water.

Nutritional Information per Serving:

Calories: 313; Total Fat: 8.5 g; Carbs: 19.2 g; Dietary Fiber: 3.2 g; Sugars: 5.8 g; Protein: 38.7 g; Cholesterol: 89 mg; Sodium: 956 mg

HCG
Beef Entrees

Roasted Beef Brisket

Yield: 1 Serving
Total Time: 8 Hours 40 Minutes
Prep Time: 10 Minutes
Cook Time: 8 Hours 30 Minutes

Ingredients

- 100 gram lean beef brisket
- 5 cloves garlic, crushed
- ¼ cup chopped red onion
- 6 stalks celery
- 1 tablespoon onion powder
- 1 tablespoon garlic powder
- Pinch of chili pepper
- Pinch of cayenne pepper
- 1 tablespoon paprika
- Pinch of salt & pepper

Directions:

In a small bowl, mix spices and rub onto beef; sprinkle with salt and place in a crockpot. Fill halfway with water and add celery; cook on high for about 30 minutes and then lower heat to cook on low for about 6-8 hours. Serve with horseradish sauce (page 47).

Phase 3 modifications: Sear meat in olive oil on high heat before cooking. Add Greek yogurt or mayonnaise to horseradish sauce.

Nutritional Information per Serving:

Calories: 281; Total Fat: 7.5 g; Carbs: 20.4 g; Dietary Fiber: 5.6 g; Sugars: 7.4 g; Protein: 34.3 g; Cholesterol: 89 mg; Sodium: 130 mg

Fajitas/ Carne Asada

Yield: 1 Serving
Total Time: 35 Minutes
Prep Time: 10 Minutes
Cook Time: 25 Minutes

Ingredients

- 100 grams sliced beef
- 2 tablespoons fresh orange juice
- 1 clove garlic chopped
- 1 red onion, chopped
- 1 cup chopped tomatoes
- 3 tablespoons lemon juice
- Pinch of cayenne pepper
- 1/8 teaspoon chili powder
- 1/8 teaspoon oregano

Directions:

Mix spices and lemon juice; add meat and marinate for a few hours before cooking; cook in a frying pan with onion and garlic, adding tomatoes during the last 5 minutes. Serve in lettuce leaf with salsa.

Phase 3 modifications: Add yellow, red and green bell peppers to fajitas and use a little oil or butter to fry. Serve with cheddar cheese, guacamole, and sour cream.

Nutritional Information per Serving:

Calories: 279; Total Fat: 7.1 g; Carbs: 19.7 g; Dietary Fiber: 4.3 g; Sugars: 11.5 g; Protein: 33.3 g; Cholesterol: 89 mg; Sodium: 89 mg

Delicious Meatloaf

Yield: 1 Serving
Total Time: 30 Minutes
Prep Time: 10 Minutes
Cook Time: 20 Minutes

Ingredients

- 100 grams Ground beef (lean) for each serving
- 1 clove minced garlic
- 1 tablespoon chopped red onion
- Bread crumbs
- 1 ketchup recipe
- ¼ teaspoon paprika
- Pinch of cayenne

Directions:

Mix ground beef, spices and chopped onion; transfer to a baking dish and baste with ketchup mixture; bake in a 350°F oven for about 15-20 minutes.

Phase 2 variations: add apple pulp for a sweeter and moist meatloaf.

Nutritional Information per Serving:

Calories: 323; Total Fat: 7.9 g; Carbs: 26.5 g; Dietary Fiber: 1.9 g; Sugars: 5.7 g; Protein: 34.8 g; Cholesterol: 89 mg; Sodium: 441 mg

Ground Beef Tacos

Yield: 1 Serving
Total Time: 35 Minutes
Prep Time: 10 Minutes
Cook Time: 25 Minutes

Ingredients

- 100 grams lean ground beef
- 1 clove garlic, minced
- ½ red onion, minced
- Lettuce leaves
- Cayenne pepper
- Fresh chopped cilantro
- Pinch of dried oregano
- Dash of onion powder
- Dash of garlic powder
- Pinch of salt & pepper

Directions:

Fry beef in a splash of lemon juice until browned; add garlic, onion and spices, and water and simmer for about 5-10 minutes. Season with salt and serve taco style in romaine lettuce or butter lettuce or with a side of salsa or tomatoes.

Phase 3 modifications: Serve with guacamole, sour cream or cheddar cheese.

Nutritional Information per Serving:

Calories: 194; Total Fat: 6.3 g; Carbs: 1.9 g; Dietary Fiber: 0.5 g; Sugars: 0.7 g; Protein: 30.6 g; Cholesterol: 89 mg; Sodium: 67 mg

Italian Veal

Yield: 1 Serving
Total Time: 30 Minutes
Prep Time: 10 Minutes
Cook Time: 20 Minutes

Ingredients

- 100 grams veal cutlet
- 1 clove garlic, minced
- ½ red onion, minced
- Bread crumbs
- 1 serving marinara sauce
- Pinch of marjoram
- 1/8 teaspoon dried oregano
- ¼ teaspoon dried basil
- Pinch of salt & pepper

Directions:

In a small bowl, mix dry spices and Melba crumbs. Dip veal in lemon juice and coat with Melba mix; fry over high heat and top with marinara. Bake in a 350°F oven for about 20 minutes. Serve garnished with remaining Melba mix, basil, salt and pepper.

Phase 3 modifications: Baste veal with olive oil and top with mozzarella or provolone cheese. Serve topped with sautéed mushrooms or grated parmesan.

Nutritional Information per Serving:

Calories: 362; Total Fat: 13.4 g; Carbs: 23.7 g; Dietary Fiber: 2 g; Sugars: 3.6 g; Protein: 34.3 g; Cholesterol: 114 mg; Sodium: 359 mg

Veal Picatta

Yield: 1 Serving
Total Time: 45 Minutes
Prep Time: 20 Minutes
Cook Time: 25 Minutes

Ingredients

- 100 grams veal cutlet
- 1 clove of garlic, minced
- Bread crumbs
- 2 tablespoons fresh lemon juice
- 2 tablespoons fresh caper juice
- ¼ cup vegetable broth
- 1 bay leaf
- Pinch of paprika
- Pinch of salt & pepper

Directions:

In a small bowl, mix paprika, Melba crumbs, salt and pepper.

Dip veal in fresh lemon juice and coat with Melba mixture; fry in a splash of lemon juice over high heat until cooked through; set aside.

Deglaze pan with caper juice, lemon juice, and vegetable broth; add bay leaf and garlic and cook for about 1-2 minutes and then discard bay leaf.

Serve veal topped with the remaining lemon sauce and garnished with lemon slices.

Phase 3 modifications: deglaze pan with about ¼ cup of white wine and melt in two tablespoons of butter; pour the sauce over veal and serve.

Nutritional Information per Serving:

Calories: 361; Total Fat: 13.4 g; Carbs: 21.5 g; Dietary Fiber: 1.5 g; Sugars: 2.6 g; Protein: 35.4 g; Cholesterol: 114 mg; Sodium: 654 mg

Veal Florentine

Yield: 1 Serving
Total Time: 50 Minutes
Prep Time: 15 Minutes
Cook Time: 35 Minutes

Ingredients

- 100 grams veal cutlet
- ½ red onion, minced
- 1 clove garlic, minced
- Bread crumbs
- 1 cup chopped Spinach
- 2 tablespoons fresh lemon juice
- ¼ cup beef broth
- 2 leaves of basil, chopped
- Pinch of paprika
- Pinch of lemon zest
- Dash of garlic powder
- Pinch of salt & pepper

Directions:

Pound veal cutlet until tender and flat. In a small bowl, mix dry spices, lemon zest, paprika and Melba toast crumbs.

Dip veal in fresh lemon juice and coat with Melba mixture; fry in a saucepan with lemon juice over high heat until cooked through and browned. Transfer meat to a plate and deglaze the pan with broth; add onion, garlic, basil and spinach; cook until spinach is wilted.

Top veal with spinach mixture; season with salt and pepper and serve garnished with lemon wedges.

Phase 3 modifications: fry spinach with olive oil and stir in parmesan and ricotta cheese. Serve veal topped with spinach mixture and parmesan cheese curls and toasted pine nuts.

Nutritional Information per Serving:

Calories: 368; Total Fat: 13.3 g; Carbs: 24.6 g; Dietary Fiber: 2.5 g; Sugars: 3.1 g; Protein: 35.4 g; Cholesterol: 114 mg; Sodium: 327 mg

Mongolian Beef w/ Cabbage

Yield: 1 Serving
Total Time: 40 Minutes
Prep Time: 10 Minutes
Cook Time: 30 Minutes

Ingredients

- 100 grams sliced Mongolian beef
- 1 tablespoon chopped green onions
- 2 cloves garlic, minced
- 1 cup chopped cabbage
- 2 tablespoons Bragg's liquid aminos
- ½ cup beef broth
- 2 tablespoons fresh lemon juice
- 3 tablespoons fresh orange juice
- 1 tablespoon apple cider vinegar
- Pinch of stevia
- ¼ teaspoon chili powder
- Pinch of salt & pepper

Directions:

In a frying pan, stir spices in liquid ingredients until dissolved; stir fry on high heat until flavors are combined and add cabbage and beef. Cook, adding more water as needed and orange slices for a sweeter taste.

Phase 3 modifications: Stir fry with veggies such as zucchini or bell pepper. Cook beef with coconut, peanut, chili or sesame oil and add soy sauce for more flavor. Serve topped with a tablespoon of crushed peanuts.

Nutritional Information per Serving:

Calories: 261; Total Fat: 7.4 g; Carbs: 11.7 g; Dietary Fiber: 2.7 g; Sugars: 7.9 g; Protein: 34.6 g; Cholesterol: 89 mg; Sodium: 477 mg

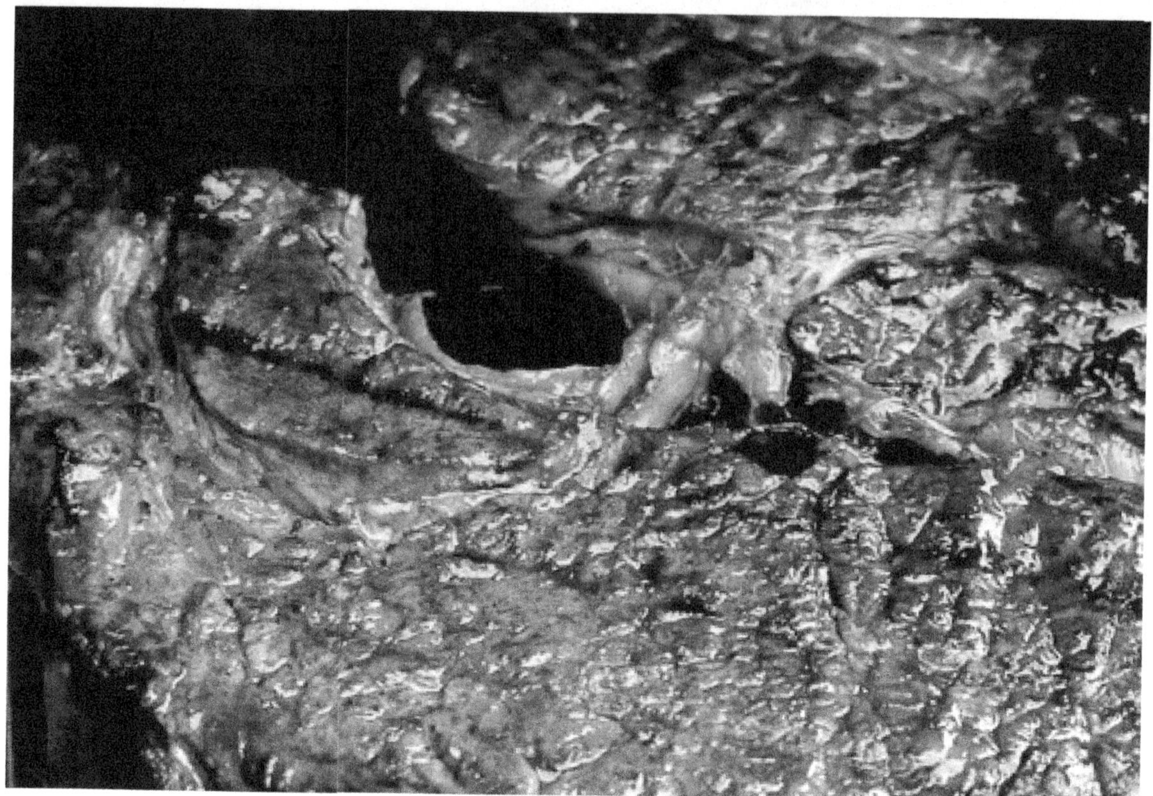

Pepper Crusted Steak

Yield: 1 Serving
Total Time: 15 Minutes
Prep Time: 10 Minutes
Cook Time: 5 Minutes

Ingredients

- 100 grams lean steak
- Dash of Worcestershire sauce
- Pinch of salt & pepper

Directions:

Pound meat until tender and flat; rub with salt and pepper and cook on high heat for about 3-5 minutes. Serve topped with Worcestershire sauce and garnished with caramelized onions.

Phase 3 modifications: Top with sautéed mushrooms in butter, onions or blue cheese.

Nutritional Information per Serving:

Calories: 189; Total Fat: 6.2 g; Carbs: 0.2 g; Dietary Fiber: 0 g; Sugars: 0.1 g; Protein: 30.4 g; Cholesterol: 89 mg; Sodium: 228 mg

Yield: 1 Serving
Total Time: 55 Minutes
Prep Time: 10 Minutes
Cook Time: 45 Minutes

Pasta-less Meat Sauce

Ingredients

- 100 grams lean ground beef
- 1 ½ red onion, minced
- 2 cloves garlic, minced
- 2 cups chopped tomatoes
- 8 ounces tomato sauce
- ½ teaspoon dried basil
- ¼ teaspoon oregano
- Pinch of stevia
- Pinch of cayenne pepper
- Pinch of salt & pepper

Directions:

Brown beef and drain excess oil; stir in garlic, onion, chopped tomatoes, tomato sauce and herbs and simmer for about 30 minutes, adding water as needed. Serve over cabbage noodles.

Phase 3 modifications: Add a dollop of olive oil or chopped black or green olives and serve topped with parmesan cheese.

Nutritional Information per Serving:

Calories: 311; Total Fat: 7.5 g; Carbs: 27.6 g; Dietary Fiber: 8.2 g; Sugars: 9.6 g; Protein: 36.7 g; Cholesterol: 89 mg; Sodium: 1272 mg

Beef Bourguignon

Yield: 1 Serving
Total Time: 45 Minutes
Prep Time: 10 Minutes
Cook Time: 35 Minutes

Ingredients

- 100 grams beef cubed
- 1 clove garlic, chopped
- 1 tablespoon chopped red onion
- 3 tablespoons tomato paste
- 1 cup beef broth
- Pinch of marjoram
- Pinch of dried thyme
- Pinch of salt & pepper

Directions:

Sauté beef along with garlic and onion; stir in remaining ingredients and cook on low heat for about 30 minutes or until beef is cooked through.

Phase 3 modifications: Whisk in butter, add non starchy veggies and ½ cup of red wine.

Nutritional Information per Serving:

Calories: 268; Total Fat: 7.9 g; Carbs: 11.1 g; Dietary Fiber: 2.3 g; Sugars: 7 g; Protein: 37.4 g; Cholesterol: 89 mg; Sodium: 877 mg

Yield: 1 Serving
Total Time: 16 Minutes
Prep Time: 10 Minutes
Cook Time: 6 Minutes

Hamburgers

Ingredients

- 100 grams lean ground hamburger
- 1 clove garlic, minced
- Pinch of garlic powder
- ½ red onion, minced
- Pinch of cayenne pepper
- Pinch of onion powder
- Pinch of salt & pepper

Directions:

In a large bowl, mix together all ingredients; form about three patties and fry them in a pan until cooked through. Cook for about 3 minutes per side, adding water as needed.

Variations: Add Bragg's, lemon juice, and stevia.

Phase 3 modifications: Add gorgonzola cheese to meat before cooking. Serve topped with chili and cheese or sautéed mushrooms and Swiss cheese.

Nutritional Information per Serving:

Calories: 197; Total Fat: 6.3 g; Carbs: 2.6 g; Dietary Fiber: 0.4 g; Sugars: 0.7 g; Protein: 30.8 g; Cholesterol: 89 mg; Sodium: 67 mg

Cabbage Rolls

Yield: 1 Serving
Total Time: 55 Minutes
Prep Time: 10 Minutes
Cook Time: 45 Minutes

Ingredients

- 100 grams lean ground beef
- 1 clove garlic, minced
- 1 tablespoon chopped red onion
- 1 cup beef broth
- Dash of onion powder
- Dash of garlic powder

Directions:

Preheat oven to 375°F. Blanch cabbage and set aside.

In a pan, cook together garlic, onion, beef and spices until beef is browned; spoon the mixture into cabbage leaves and roll up the burrito style. Place the rolls in a baking dish and add broth; bake for about 20-30 minutes, spooning sauce over the rolls severally to keep them moist.

Nutritional Information per Serving:

Calories: 230; Total Fat: 7.6 g; Carbs: 2.3 g; Dietary Fiber: 0.3 g; Sugars: 1.3 g; Protein: 35.4 g; Cholesterol: 89 mg; Sodium: 830 mg

Gingered Beef

Yield: 1 Serving
Total Time: 25 Minutes
Prep Time: 10 Minutes
Cook Time: 15 Minutes

Ingredients

- 100 grams beef, sliced thinly into strips
- ¼ teaspoon fresh grated ginger
- 1 clove garlic, minced
- 1-2 tablespoons chopped green onions
- 2 tablespoons fresh lemon juice
- 2 tablespoons pure apple cider vinegar
- 2 tablespoons Bragg's liquid aminos
- ¼ cup beef broth
- Pinch of salt & pepper
- Pinch of stevia

Directions:

Cook spices and ginger in broth until fragrant; stir in beef and cook for a few minutes, deglazing pan with water. Serve hot topped with green onions.

Nutritional Information per Serving:

Calories: 213; Total Fat: 6.9 g; Carbs: 2 g; Dietary Fiber: 0.4 g; Sugars: 1.1 g; Protein: 32 g; Cholesterol: 89 mg; Sodium: 265 mg

Italian Beef Rolls

Yield: 1 Serving
Total Time: 45 Minutes
Prep Time: 10 Minutes
Cook Time: 35 Minutes

Ingredients

- 100 grams lean flank steak
- 1 tablespoon chopped red onion
- 1 clove garlic, minced
- 1 cup finely chopped cabbage
- 2 tablespoons Bragg's liquid aminos
- 2 tablespoons apple cider vinegar
- 1 cup beef broth
- 1 teaspoon Italian herb mix
- Pinch of salt & pepper

Directions:

Pound meat until tender and flat.

Cook cabbage, vinegar, spices and Bragg's until tender; spoon the mixture onto meat and roll up to make a wrap. Add to a pan and add in broth; season with salt and spices and bake in a 375°F oven for about 20 minutes or until meat is cooked through and cabbage is tender.

Variations: Use spinach instead pf cabbage.

Phase 3 modifications: Top the rolls with marinara sauce, herbed cream cheese, provolone cheese or Alfredo sauce and bake until browned and bubbly.

Nutritional Information per Serving:

Calories: 196; Total Fat: 5.9 g; Carbs: 7.3 g; Dietary Fiber: 2.5 g; Sugars: 4.1 g; Protein: 6.1 g; Cholesterol: 49 mg; Sodium: 857 mg

Corned Beef w/ Cabbage

Yield: 1 Serving
Total Time: 1 Hour 25 Minutes
Prep Time: 10 Minutes
Cook Time: 1 Hour 15 Minutes

Ingredients

- 100 gram lean beef
- ½ cup apple cider vinegar
- 1 cup chopped cabbage
- ½ onion red chopped
- 1 teaspoon whole black peppercorns
- Pinch of allspice
- ¼ teaspoon fresh thyme
- 1 teaspoon powdered mustard
- 1 bay leaf
- Liquid smoke
- Pinch of salt & pepper

Directions:

Sprinkle beef with salt, pepper and mustard and add to a crock pot along with spices and onion; cover with water and stir in vinegar. Bring the mixture to a boil; lower heat and simmer for about 1 hour. Skim off excess fat and stir in cabbage; cook for another 1 hour or until cabbage and meat are tender. Slice meat thinly and serve with horseradish sauce.

Nutritional Information per Serving:

Calories: 257; Total Fat: 6.5 g; Carbs: 12.2 g; Dietary Fiber: 3.7 g; Sugars: 5.1 g; Protein: 32.1 g; Cholesterol: 89 mg; Sodium: 88 mg

Corned Beef Hash

Yield: 1 Serving
Total Time: 22 Minutes
Prep Time: 10 Minutes
Cook Time: 12 Minutes

Ingredients

- Leftover corned beef from corned beef and cabbage
- 1 clove garlic, minced
- ½ red onion, minced
- 1 cup chopped cabbage
- Pinch of fresh chopped oregano
- Pinch of fresh thyme
- Pinch of salt & pepper

Directions:

Thinly chop beef into chunks and combine with cabbage.

Preheat a nonstick skillet and press in beef mixture; cover and cook over medium heat for about 5-6 minutes or until lightly browned, adding splashes of beef broth to deglaze. Stir to mix well and press the mixture down again and continue cooking for another 5-6 minutes; repeat until browned.

Phase 3 modifications: brown beef in butter and add bell peppers and other veggies.

Nutritional Information per Serving:

Calories: 208; Total Fat: 6.3 g; Carbs: 5.3 g; Dietary Fiber: 2.1 g; Sugars: 2.7 g; Protein: 31.4 g; Cholesterol: 89 mg; Sodium: 79 mg

Italian Baked Meatballs

Yield: 1 Serving
Total Time: 40 Minutes
Prep Time: 10 Minutes
Cook Time: 30 Minutes

Ingredients

- 100 grams lean ground beef
- 1 clove garlic, minced
- ½ red onion, minced
- 1/8 teaspoon oregano
- 1/8 teaspoon garlic powder
- 1/8 teaspoon oregano
- ¼ teaspoon basil
- Bread crumbs
- 1 serving marinara sauce

Directions:

In a large bowl, mix together spices, crumbs and beef and roll into small balls; place them in a baking dish and top with marinara sauce. Bake in a 350°F oven for about 20-30 minutes. Serve the meatballs hot over cabbage noodles garnished with fresh basil.

Phase 3 modifications: Top with mozzarella or provolone cheese and bake until browned and bubbly; serve topped with parmesan.

Nutritional Information per Serving:

Calories: 301; Total Fat: 9.6 g; Carbs: 18.6 g; Dietary Fiber: 3.7 g; Sugars: 1.6 g; Protein: 32.8 g; Cholesterol: 92 mg; Sodium: 570 mg

Herbed London Broil

Yield: 1 Serving
Total Time: 40 Minutes
Prep Time: 10 Minutes
Cook Time: 30 Minutes

Ingredients

- 100 grams lean London broil, sliced thinly into strips
- 1 clove garlic, minced
- 1 red onion, minced
- ¼ cup beef broth or water
- Chopped Italian parsley
- Pinch of rosemary
- 1/8 teaspoon thyme
- Pinch of salt & pepper

Directions:

Coat beef with salt and pepper and add to a pan along with beef broth and herbs; cook until beef is cooked through. Serve garnished with parsley.

Nutritional Information per Serving:

Calories: 201; Total Fat: 6.6 g; Carbs: 1.4 g; Dietary Fiber: 0.4 g; Sugars: 0.6 g; Protein: 31.7 g; Cholesterol: 89 mg; Sodium: 257 mg

Tasty Sloppy Joes

Yield: 1 Serving
Total Time: 30 Minutes
Prep Time: 10 Minutes
Cook Time: 20 Minutes

Ingredients

- 100 grams beef, ground
- 1 serving barbeque sauce
- Butter lettuce leaves

Directions:

Brown beef and add water and barbecue sauce; cook for about 5 minutes and serve on lettuce leaves.

Brown ground beef in small frying pan. Add barbeque sauce and a little

Phase 3 modifications: Serve topped with caramelized onion rings, stevia and cheddar cheese slices.

Nutritional Information per Serving:

Calories: 200; Total Fat: 6.3 g; Carbs: 3.4 g; Dietary Fiber: 0.1 g; Sugars: 2.4 g; Protein: 30.3 g; Cholesterol: 89 mg; Sodium: 170 mg

Baked Stuffed Tomatoes

Yield: 1 Serving
Total Time: 55 Minutes
Prep Time: 10 Minutes
Cook Time: 45 Minutes

Ingredients

- 100 grams ground beef
- 1 clove garlic, minced
- ½ red onion, minced
- Bread crumbs
- 2 medium tomatoes, hollowed out
- Pinch of cayenne pepper
- 1/8 teaspoon onion powder
- 1/8 teaspoon garlic powder
- Pinch of salt & pepper

Directions:

Sprinkle tomatoes with salt and turn upside down to drain for at least 10 minutes; brown beef, onion, garlic and spices and spoon into tomatoes. Place tomatoes in a baking dish and add water to the bottom; bake in a 350°F oven for about 20 minutes. Serve garnished with parsley.

Nutritional Information per Serving:

Calories: 349; Total Fat: 8.3 g; Carbs: 31.6 g; Dietary Fiber: 4.6 g; Sugars: 8.9 g; Protein: 36.5 g; Cholesterol: 89 mg; Sodium: 289 mg

Roasted Beef & Apple Kabobs

Yield: 1 Serving
Total Time: 40 Minutes
Prep Time: 10 Minutes
Cook Time: 30 Minutes

Ingredients

- 100 grams of lean beef, diced
- ¼ onion petals
- 1 apple, diced
- 1 tablespoon Bragg's liquid aminos
- 3 tablespoons apple cider vinegar
- ½ cup beef broth
- Pinch of stevia

Directions:

Marinate meat in vinegar, broth and spices and arrange it alternatively on skewers with onion petals and apple. Barbecue until cooked through, basting frequently with the remaining marinade. Heat the remaining marinade until thick and use it as a dipping sauce.

Nutritional Information per Serving:

Calories: 330; Total Fat: 7.3 g; Carbs: 31.7 g; Dietary Fiber: 5.4 g; Sugars: 23.7 g; Protein: 33.4 g; Cholesterol: 89 mg; Sodium: 452 mg

Stuffed Chard Rolls

Yield: 1 Serving
Total Time: 45 Minutes
Prep Time: 10 Minutes
Cook Time: 35 Minutes

Ingredients

- 100 grams lean ground beef
- 1 clove of garlic, minced
- ½ red onion, minced
- 1 serving marinara sauce
- 1 large chard leaves
- Pinch of cayenne pepper
- 1/8 teaspoon garlic powder
- 1/8 teaspoon onion powder
- 1/8 teaspoon oregano
- 1/8 teaspoon basil
- Pinch of salt & pepper

Directions:

Brown beef, onion, garlic and spices in a splash of water and transfer the mixture to chard leaf; wrap and place on a baking dish. Cover with broth and bake in a 350°F oven for about 20 minutes. Serve garnished with parsley or fresh spices.

Nutritional Information per Serving:

Calories: 302; Total Fat: 9.7 g; Carbs: 18.9 g; Dietary Fiber: 3.7 g; Sugars: 11.7 g; Protein: 32.8 g; Cholesterol: 92 mg; Sodium: 579 mg

Yield: 8 Servings

Total Time: 45 Minutes

Prep Time: 10 Minutes

Cook Time: 35 Minutes

Beef Chili

Ingredients

- 2 pounds lean ground beef
- 2 (15-ounce) cans diced tomatoes
- 2 teaspoons chili powder
- ½ teaspoon cumin
- 1 teaspoon garlic powder
- 1 teaspoon onion powder
- 1 cup water
- Pinch of salt & pepper
- Toast

Directions:

In a saucepan, brown beef and rinse with hot water in a colander; return to pan and stir in the remaining ingredients. Bring to a gentle boil; lower heat and simmer for about 20 minutes. Serve right away with Melba toast. Store excess chili in a freezer.

Variation: use ground turkey or chicken in place of ground beef.

Nutritional Information per Serving:

Calories: 235; Total Fat: 7.4 g; Carbs: 5.1 g; Dietary Fiber: 1.6 g; Sugars: 3.1 g; Protein: 35.5 g; Cholesterol: 101 mg; Sodium: 88 mg

Delicious Beef Jerky

Yield: 4 Servings
Total Time: 40 Minutes
Prep Time: 10 Minutes
Cook Time: 30 Minutes

Ingredients

- 12 ounces lean top round, thinly sliced
- Pinch of garlic powder
- Pinch of cayenne powder
- Pinch of salt & pepper

Directions:

Rub spices into beef slices and place in dehydrator; set to beef jerky. When ready to serve, divide beef jerky into four servings.

Nutritional Information per Serving:

Calories: 158; Total Fat: 5.3 g; Carbs: 0 g; Dietary Fiber: 0 g; Sugars: 0 g; Protein: 25.8 g; Cholesterol: 76 mg; Sodium: 56 mg

Yield: 1 Serving
Total Time: 40 Minutes
Prep Time: 10 Minutes
Cook Time: 30 Minutes

Chinese Steak

Ingredients

- 3 ounces Steak, diced
- 5 tablespoons Vegetable Broth
- 3 ounces shredded Cabbage
- 1 clove Garlic, Minced
- ½ packet Stevia
- Dash of Onion Powder
- Dash of Chinese 5 Spice
- Dash of Sea Salt
- Dash of Pepper

Directions:

Add a tablespoon of broth to a saucepan and sauté garlic; stir in cabbage and 2 tablespoons of broth. Cook for a few minutes and remove cabbage from heat when it is still crunchy. Add the remaining ingredients to a pan and stir fry; return cabbage and cook for about 1-2 minutes.

Variations: use shrimp or chicken instead of steak.

Nutritional Information per Serving:

Calories: 208; Total Fat: 4.8 g; Carbs: 6.5 g; Dietary Fiber: 2.2 g; Sugars: 3.1 g; Protein: 33.6 g; Cholesterol: 77 mg; Sodium: 527 mg

Fajitas/ Carne Asada

Yield: 4 Servings
Total Time: 40 Minutes
Prep Time: 10 Minutes
Cook Time: 30 Minutes

Ingredients

- 1 pound lean ground beef
- 1 ½ cups water
- 3 cups chopped tomatoes
- ½ cup chopped red onion
- 4 cloves garlic, minced
- 1 teaspoon chili powder
- ½ teaspoon oregano
- Cayenne Pepper
- Pinch of salt & pepper
- Lettuce Leaves

Directions:

In a saucepan, brown onions and beef; drain and rinse. Stir in the remaining ingredients and simmer for about 20 minutes; transfer the mixture to lettuce and roll to wrap.

Variation: use ground turkey or chicken instead of ground beef.

Nutritional Information per Serving:

Calories: 253; Total Fat: 7.5 g; Carbs: 9.4 g; Dietary Fiber: 2.6 g; Sugars: 4.8 g; Protein: 36.2 g; Cholesterol: 101 mg; Sodium: 92 mg

Yield: 2 Servings
Total Time: 15 Minutes
Prep Time: 10 Minutes
Cook Time: 5 Minutes

Burger

Ingredients

- 6 ounces ground beef
- 1 sweet onion
- 1 tomato, thickly sliced
- 4 lettuce leaves

Directions:

Form ground beef into two patties and top each with onions and tomatoes; grill for about 5 minutes. Sandwich each patty with onions and tomatoes between two lettuce leaves and serve.

Variation: use chicken instead of beef.

Nutritional Information per Serving:

Calories: 187; Total Fat: 5.4 g; Carbs: 6.7 g; Dietary Fiber: 1.6 g; Sugars: 3.3 g; Protein: 26.7 g; Cholesterol: 76 mg; Sodium: 60 mg

Tasty Crock Pot Roast

Yield: 5 Servings
Total Time: 10 Hours 10 Minutes
Prep Time: 10 Minutes
Cook Time: 10 Hours

Ingredients

- 1 pound lean roast
- 1 onion, chopped
- 1 celery stalk
- ½ cup water
- 1 clove garlic, minced
- sea salt
- pepper
- Chinese spice blend
- 1 head lettuce

Directions:

Combine all ingredients in a crock pot and cook on low for about 8-10 hours. Roll the mixture onto lettuce leaf and wrap. Serve.

Variation: serve the mixture over shredded lettuce.

Nutritional Information per Serving:

Calories: 179; Total Fat: 5.7 g; Carbs: 2.4 g; Dietary Fiber: 0.5 g; Sugars: 1 g; Protein: 27.8 g; Cholesterol: 81 mg; Sodium: 64 mg

Fish & Seafood Entrees

Spiced Shrimp with Tomatoes

Yield: 1 Serving
Total Time: 20 Minutes
Prep Time: 10 Minutes
Cook Time: 10 Minutes

Ingredients

- 100 grams shrimp
- 1 clove garlic, minced
- ½ red onion, minced
- ½ cup vegetable broth or water
- 2 tomatoes chopped
- Pinch of stevia
- Pinch of allspice
- 1/8 teaspoon garlic powder
- 1/8 teaspoon onion powder
- 1/8 teaspoon curry

Directions:

Sauté shrimp with onion and garlic for about 3 minute for until cooked through; stir in stevia, curry and broth, onion powder and garlic powder and cook for about 5-10 minutes.

Nutritional Information per Serving:

Calories: 146; Total Fat: 2.4 g; Carbs: 3.7 g; Dietary Fiber: 0.4 g; Sugars: 1 g; Protein: 25.4 g; Cholesterol: 211 mg; Sodium: 627 mg

Shrimp Etouffee

Yield: 1 Serving

Total Time: 45 Minutes

Prep Time: 10 Minutes

Cook Time: 35 Minutes

Ingredients

- 100 grams shrimp
- 1 tablespoon chopped green onion
- 1 tablespoon chopped red onion
- 1 clove garlic, minced
- 4 stalks celery, chopped
- ½ cup vegetable broth
- Pinch of cayenne pepper
- Pinch of thyme
- Pinch of salt & pepper

Directions:

Mix veggies and spices and simmer for about 15 minutes or until celery is tender; add shrimp and cook for about 10-20 minutes. Serve hot.

Phase 3 modifications: stir in browned butter and dry sherry for a richer flavorful sauce.

Nutritional Information per Serving:

Calories: 145; Total Fat: 2.4 g; Carbs: 3.5 g; Dietary Fiber: 0.5 g; Sugars: 0.9 g; Protein: 25.4 g; Cholesterol: 211 mg; Sodium: 627 mg

Scrumptious Shrimp

Yield: 1 Serving
Total Time: 30 Minutes
Prep Time: 10 Minutes
Cook Time: 20 Minutes

Ingredients

- 3 ounces shrimp, diced
- 5 tablespoons vegetable broth
- 1 clove garlic, minced
- 3 ounces shredded cabbage
- Dash of Chinese 5 Spice
- dash of onion powder
- ½ packet stevia
- Pinch of salt & pepper

Directions:

Add a tablespoon of broth to a pan and sauté garlic; stir in cabbage and two tablespoons of broth. Cook over medium heat for a few minutes; transfer cabbage to a plate while still crunchy and stir the remaining ingredients in the pan; stir fry and return cabbage. Cook for about 1-2 minutes.

Variations: use chicken of steak instead of shrimp.

Nutritional Information per Serving:

Calories: 140: Total Fat: 2 g; Carbs: 7.8 g; Dietary Fiber: 2.2 g; Sugars: 3.1 g; Protein: 22.2 g; Cholesterol: 179 mg; Sodium: 696 mg

Grilled Fish & Red Onions

Yield: 1 Serving
Total Time: 15 Minutes
Prep Time: 10 Minutes
Cook Time: 5 Minutes

Ingredients

- 3 ounces fish filet
- 4 onion slices
- Pinch of garlic powder
- Pinch of salt & pepper

Directions:

Place fish filet on grill and arrange onion slices on top; season with garlic powder, salt and pepper and grill for about 5 minutes or until fish is cooked through.

Variation: use chicken in place of fish.

Nutritional Information per Serving:

Calories: 157; Total Fat: 6.4 g; Carbs: 17.1 g; Dietary Fiber: 1.4 g; Sugars: 2.9 g; Protein: 8.2 g; Cholesterol: 18 mg; Sodium: 737 mg

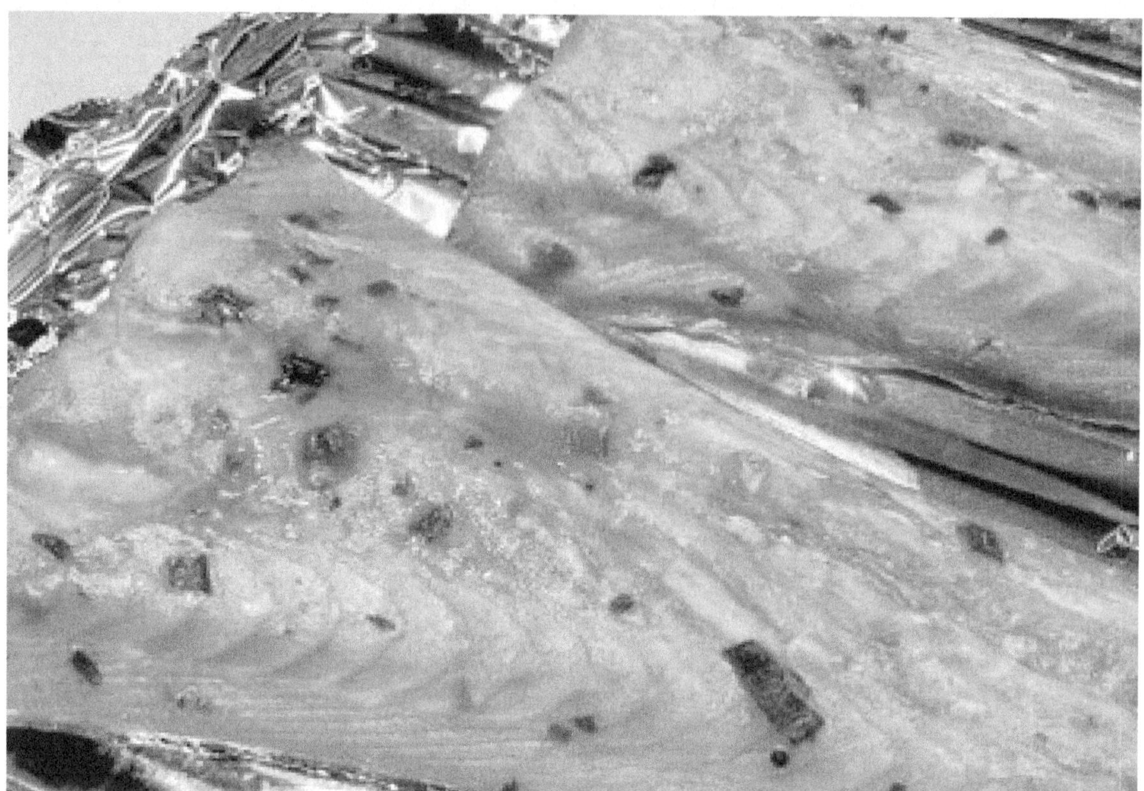

Citrus Baked Fish

Yield: 1 Serving
Total Time: 25 Minutes
Prep Time: 10 Minutes
Cook Time: 15 Minutes

Ingredients

- 3 ounces white fish
- 2 tablespoons fresh lemon juice
- Pinch of salt & pepper

Directions:

Place fish on an aluminum foil.

In a small bowl, mix fresh lemon juice, salt and pepper; pour over fish and bake in a 350°F oven for about 15 minutes or until fish is cooked through.

Nutritional Information per Serving:

Calories 82: Total Fat 1.2g: Carb 1.1g: Dietary Fiber 0.2g: Sugars 1g: Protein 16.2g Cholesterol 41mg: Sodium 508mg

Fried Fish

Yield: 1 Serving
Total Time: 15 Minutes
Prep Time: 10 Minutes
Cook Time: 5 Minutes

Ingredients

- 3 ounces Fish
- 1 tablespoon Milk
- 1 Melba Toast, crushed
- Pinch of salt & pepper

Directions:

Mix crushed toast with seasonings; dip fish in milk and then coat with toast mix. Grill for about 5 minutes.

Variation: replace fish with chicken.

Nutritional Information per Serving:

Calories: 205; Total Fat: 0.8 g; Carbs: 15.2 g; Dietary Fiber: 0.5 g; Sugars: 0.7 g; Protein: 13 g; Cholesterol: 30 mg; Sodium: 460 mg

Breaded Tilapia

Yield: 2 Servings
Total Time: 15 Minutes
Prep Time: 10 Minutes
Cook Time: 5 Minutes

Ingredients

- 8 ounce tilapia
- 4 tablespoons fresh lemon juice
- 2 rounds Melba toast, crushed
- Pinch of onion powder
- Pinch of salt & pepper

Directions:

In a small bowl, mix crushed toast, onion powder, salt and pepper.

Drizzle lemon juice over fish and coat with toast mix. Grill for about 5 minutes.

Variation: replace fish with 6 ounces of chicken breast.

Nutritional Information per Serving:

Calories: 141; Total Fat: 1.6 g; Carbs: 9.1 g; Dietary Fiber: 0.4 g; Sugars: 0.8 g; Protein: 22.5 g; Cholesterol: 55 mg; Sodium: 163 mg

Mushroom Fish Filet

Yield: 3 Servings
Total Time: 25 Minutes
Prep Time: 10 Minutes
Cook Time: 15 Minutes

Ingredients

- 9 ounces tilapia fillet
- 8 ounces cream of mushroom soup (low-fat)
- Pinch of salt & pepper
- cooking spray

Directions:

Lightly grease a baking pan; place fish in the pan and season with salt and pepper. Cover with mushroom soup and marinate for about 2 hours; bake in a 350°F oven for about 15 minutes. Remove fish from oven and discard soup, scraping off soup from fish.

Nutritional Information per Serving:

Calories: 136; Total Fat: 5.4 g; Carbs: 5.1 g; Dietary Fiber: 0 g; Sugars: 1.1 g; Protein: 17 g; Cholesterol: 41 mg; Sodium: 518 mg

Seafood Gumbo

Yield: 1 Serving
Total Time: 35 Minutes
Prep Time: 10 Minutes
Cook Time: 25 Minutes

Ingredients

- 3 ounces shrimp, diced
- 1 clove garlic, chopped
- 2 roma tomatoes, chopped
- ¼ teaspoon onion powder
- ¼ teaspoon tony chachere's creole seasoning
- pinch of garlic powder
- pinch of celery salt
- pinch of cayenne pepper
- 1 packet stevia

Directions:

Brown seafood in a saucepan and add the remaining ingredients; simmer for about 15 minutes.

Variation: replace seafood with chicken breast.

Nutritional Information per Serving:

Calories: 162; Total Fat: 2 g; Carbs: 12.3 g; Dietary Fiber: 3 g; Sugars: 6.7 g; Protein: 21.8 g; Cholesterol: 79 mg; Sodium: 220 mg

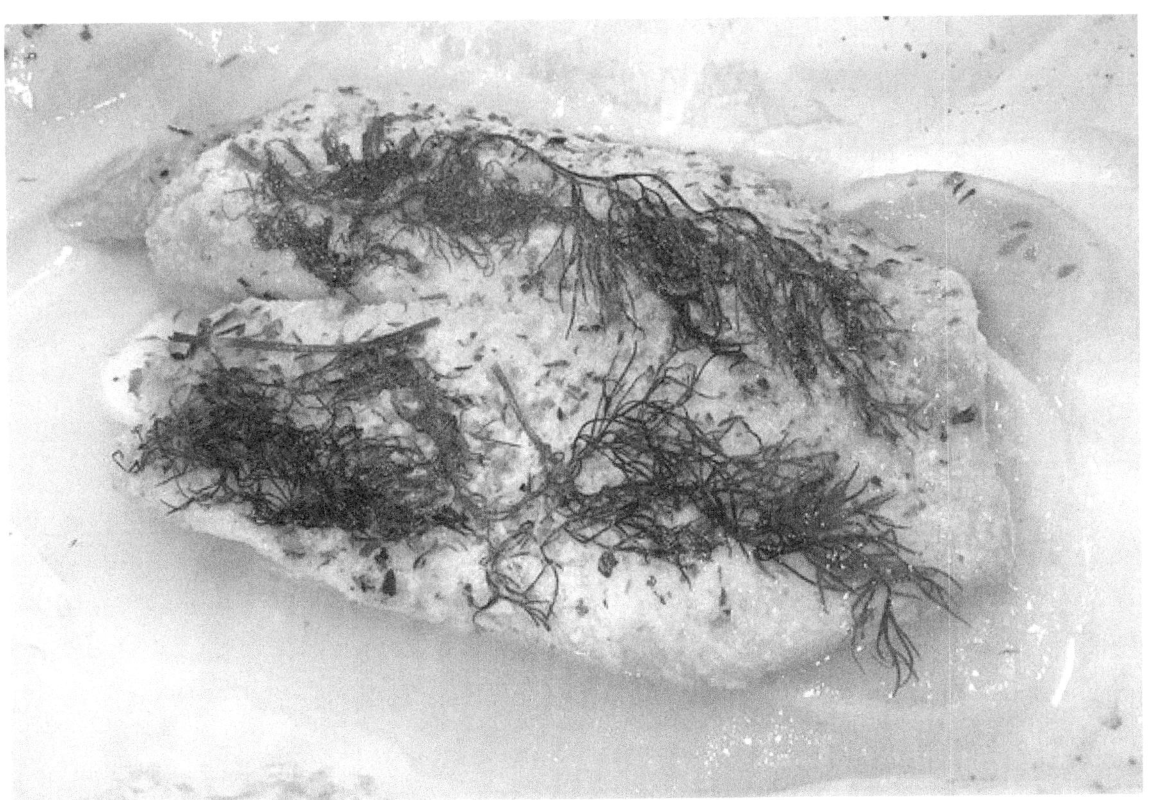

Tilapia with Herbs

Yield: 1 Serving
Total Time: 25 Minutes
Prep Time: 10 Minutes
Cook Time: 15 Minutes

Ingredients

- 100 grams of Tilapia fish
- 1 tablespoon chopped red onion
- 1 clove garlic, minced
- 2 tablespoons fresh lemon juice
- Fresh parsley
- Pinch of dill
- Pinch of salt & pepper

Directions:

Sauté fish in a splash of fresh lemon juice and water; stir in garlic, onion and fresh herbs and cook until fish is cooked through. Serve garnished with parsley.

Nutritional Information per Serving:

Calories: 104; Total Fat: 1.2 g; Carbs: 3.7 g; Dietary Fiber: 0.4 g; Sugars: 1.1 g; Protein: 19 g; Cholesterol: 49 mg; Sodium: 42 mg

Baked Curried Fish

Yield: 1 Serving
Total Time: 35 Minutes
Prep Time: 10 Minutes
Cook Time: 25 Minutes

Ingredients

- Any white fish
- 1 clove garlic, minced
- 1 tablespoon chopped red onion
- 2 tablespoons fresh lemon juice
- Bread crumbs
- Fresh parsley
- 1/8 teaspoon curry powder
- 1/8 teaspoon garlic powder
- 1/8 teaspoon onion powder
- Pinch of salt & pepper

Directions:

In a bowl, mix crumbs and dry spices; coat fish with mixture and broil until cooked through and the outside is browned. Serve garnished with fresh parsley and lemon slices.

Nutritional Information per Serving:

Calories: 163; Total Fat: 2.1 g; Carbs: 4.9 g; Dietary Fiber: 1.1 g; Sugars: 2.4 g; Protein: 21 g; Cholesterol: 49 mg; Sodium: 213 mg

Poached Halibut

Yield: 1 Serving
Total Time: 20 Minutes
Prep Time: 10 Minutes
Cook Time: 10 Minutes

Ingredients

- 100 grams halibut
- 1 clove garlic, minced
- 1 tablespoon chopped red onion
- ½ teaspoon fresh ginger
- 1 tablespoon fresh lemon juice
- Pinch of grated orange zest
- ½ cup vegetable broth
- Pinch of salt & pepper
- Pinch of stevia

Directions:

In a pan, heat broth and stir in garlic, onion, lemon juice and spices; poach fish for about 5-10 minutes or until cooked through. Serve topped with cooking juices.

Nutritional Information per Serving:

Calories: 121; Total Fat: 2.4 g; Carbs: 2.7 g; Dietary Fiber: 0.6 g; Sugars: 1.1 g; Protein: 21.5 g; Cholesterol: 211 mg; Sodium: 542 mg

Creole Shrimp

Yield: 1 Serving
Total Time: 25 Minutes
Prep Time: 10 Minutes
Cook Time: 15 Minutes

Ingredients

- 100 grams shrimp
- ½ red onion, minced
- 1 clove garlic, minced
- ½ cup vegetable broth
- ¼ teaspoon horseradish sauce
- 2 tablespoons fresh lemon juice
- 1-2 teaspoons hot sauce
- Pinch of cayenne pepper
- 1/8 teaspoon onion powder
- 1/8 teaspoon garlic powder
- Pinch of thyme
- Dash of liquid smoke flavoring
- Dash of sassafras powder
- 1 bay leaf
- Pinch of salt & pepper

Directions:

In a pan, mix garlic, onion, spices and liquid ingredients; simmer for about 10 minutes. Add shrimp and continue cooking for 5 minutes more; season with salt and pepper and serve hot over a salad.

Nutritional Information per Serving:

Calories: 154; Total Fat: 2.7 g; Carbs: 3.7 g; Dietary Fiber: 0.64.5; Sugars: 1.8 g; Protein: 25.7 g; Cholesterol: 211 mg; Sodium: 763 mg

Sweet Ginger Shrimp

Yield: 1 Serving
Total Time: 25 Minutes
Prep Time: 10 Minutes
Cook Time: 15 Minutes

Ingredients

- 100 grams shrimp
- 2 tablespoons Bragg's liquid aminos
- 2 tablespoons orange juice
- 2 tablespoons fresh lemon juice
- ¼ cup vegetable broth
- Pinch of stevia
- Dash of onion powder
- Dash of garlic powder
- Pinch of chili powder
- ¼ teaspoon ginger
- Pinch of salt & pepper

Directions:

Mix spices and liquid ingredients and add shrimp; cook until shrimp is cooked through.

Nutritional Information per Serving:

Calories: 155; Total Fat: 2.4 g; Carbs: 3.7 g; Dietary Fiber: 0.4 g; Sugars: 3.7 g; Protein: 24.6 g; Cholesterol: 211 mg; Sodium: 4456 mg

Jambalaya

Yield: 1 Serving
Total Time: 55 Minutes
Prep Time: 10 Minutes
Cook Time: 45 Minutes

Ingredients

- 100 grams shrimp
- 1 clove garlic, minced
- 1 tablespoon chopped red onion
- 2 tomatoes, chopped
- 1 tablespoon fresh lemon juice
- 1 cup vegetable broth or water
- Pinch of thyme
- 1/8 teaspoon onion powder
- 1/8 teaspoon garlic powder
- Pinch of cayenne
- Dash of liquid smoke
- Dash of hot sauce
- Dash of Worcestershire sauce
- Pinch of salt & pepper
- Water

Directions:

Sauté shrimp with onion, garlic, tomatoes or celery in lemon juice until lightly browned; stir in broth and seasonings and simmer for about 20-30 minutes.

Phase 3 modifications: Add more seafood, chopped green and red bell pepper.

Nutritional Information per Serving:

Calories: 199; Total Fat: 3.5 g; Carbs: 9.2 g; Dietary Fiber: 1.9 g; Sugars: 5 g; Protein: 29.1 g; Cholesterol: 211 mg; Sodium: 1040 mg

Pepper Sautéed Shrimp

Yield: 1 Serving

Total Time: 25 Minutes

Prep Time: 10 Minutes

Cook Time: 15 Minutes

Ingredients

- 100 grams shrimp
- 1 tablespoon fresh caper juice
- 2 tablespoons fresh lemon juice
- Bread crumbs
- Pinch of salt & pepper

Directions:

Mix crumbs, salt and pepper and rub over shrimp; fry on high heat in a splash of lemon juice until shrimp is cooked through. Serve hot garnished with lemon slices and sprinkled with more pepper.

Nutritional Information per Serving:

Calories: 193; Total Fat: 2.8 g; Carbs: 4.6 g; Dietary Fiber: 0.7 g; Sugars: 1.7 g; Protein: 24.9 g; Cholesterol: 211 mg; Sodium: 420 mg

Tasty Crab Cakes

Yield: 1 Serving
Total Time: 30 Minutes
Prep Time: 10 Minutes
Cook Time: 20 Minutes

Ingredients

- 100 grams crab meat
- 1 clove garlic, minced
- ½ red onion, minced
- 1 teaspoon apple cider vinegar
- 1 tablespoon fresh lemon juice
- Bread crumbs
- Pinch of cayenne
- 1/8 teaspoon garlic powder
- 1/8 teaspoon onion powder
- Pinch of salt & pepper

Directions:

Combine all ingredients and form into cakes; press the cakes in muffin tins and bake in a 350°F oven for about 10-20 minutes or until lightly browned.

Serve over green salad.

Phase 3 modifications: Add egg to crab mixture and fry in oil or butter; serve with mayonnaise or Cajun spiced cream sauce.

Nutritional Information per Serving:

Calories: 68; Total Fat: 2.8 g; Carbs: 16.4 g; Dietary Fiber: 1 g; Sugars: 2.1 g; Protein: 4.8 g; Cholesterol: 54 mg; Sodium: 799 mg

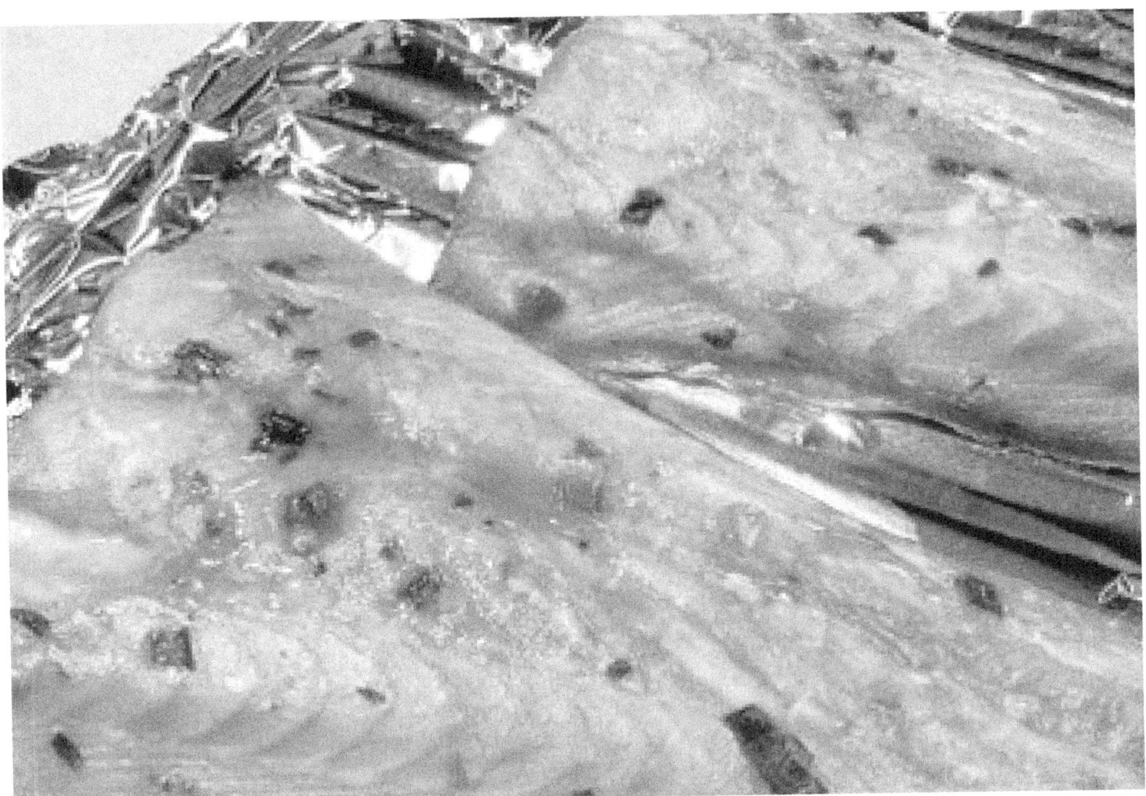

Yield: 1 Serving

Total Time: 30 Minutes

Prep Time: 10 Minutes

Cook Time: 20 Minutes

Cajun Baked Fish

Ingredients

- 100 grams white fish
- Bread crumbs
- Pinch of thyme
- Pinch of cayenne pepper to taste
- 1/8 teaspoon garlic powder
- 1/8 teaspoon onion powder
- Pinch of salt & pepper

Directions:

Mix Melba and spices; dip fish in lemon juice and coat with Melba mix. Bake in a 350°F oven for about 20 minutes or until browned. Serve garnished with parsley.

Phase 3 modifications: Dip fish into and fry in oil; serve with Cajun spiced cream sauce.

Nutritional Information per Serving:

Calories: 110; Total Fat: 1.3 g; Carbs: 5.3 g; Dietary Fiber: 0.4 g; Sugars: 0.6 g; Protein: 19.4 g; Cholesterol: 49 mg; Sodium: 252 mg

Citrus Dill Fish

Yield: 1 Serving
Total Time: 25 Minutes
Prep Time: 10 Minutes
Cook Time: 15 Minutes

Ingredients

- 100 grams white fish
- ½ red onion, minced
- 1 clove garlic, minced
- 1 teaspoon fresh dill
- 1 teaspoon apple cider vinegar
- ¼ cup vegetable broth
- 4 tablespoons fresh lemon juice
- Pinch of salt & pepper

Directions:

Sauté fish in vinegar, broth and lemon juice; stir in dill, onion and garlic and cook for 5-10 minutes or until cooked through. Serve garnished with lemon wedges.

Nutritional Information per Serving:

Calories: 124; Total Fat: 1.8 g; Carbs: 3.1 g; Dietary Fiber: 0.6 g; Sugars: 1.9 g; Protein: 20.6 g; Cholesterol: 49 mg; Sodium: 241 mg

Italian-Style Shrimp with Tomatoes

Yield: 1 Serving
Total Time: 35 Minutes
Prep Time: 10 Minutes
Cook Time: 25 Minutes

Ingredients

- 100 grams shrimp
- 2 cloves garlic, minced
- 2 large tomatoes, chopped
- 2 tablespoons fresh lemon juice
- ¼ cup vegetable broth
- Pinch of red pepper flakes
- Pinch of dried oregano
- ¼ teaspoon dried basil
- Pinch of salt & pepper

Directions:

Sauté garlic, onion and spices in lemon juice and broth; stir in tomatoes and shrimp and cook until shrimp is cooked through.

Phase 3 modifications: Cook with olive oil and add zucchini or other veggies. Serve topped with parmesan.

Nutritional Information per Serving:

Calories: 203; Total Fat: 3.1 g; Carbs: 16.9 g; Dietary Fiber: 4.7 g; Sugars: 0.4 g; Protein: 27.5 g; Cholesterol: 211 mg; Sodium: 459 mg

Tasty Wasabi Sautéed Shrimp

Yield: 1 Serving
Total Time: 25 Minutes
Prep Time: 10 Minutes
Cook Time: 15 Minutes

Ingredients

- 100 grams shrimp
- ½ red onion, minced
- 1 serving sweet wasabi marinade
- Pinch of dried ginger powder
- Pinch of stevia

Directions:

Cook onion and shrimp in wasabi marinade and serve hot over mixed green salad.

Nutritional Information per Serving:

Calories: 194; Total Fat: .71 g; Carbs: 12.69 g; Dietary Fiber: 2.2 g; Sugars: 7.4 g; Protein: 22.9 g; Cholesterol: 211 mg; Sodium: 244 mg

Spiced Mustard Shrimp w/ Chard

Yield: 1 Serving
Total Time: 30 Minutes
Prep Time: 10 Minutes
Cook Time: 20 Minutes

Ingredients

- 100 grams shrimp
- 2 cloves garlic, sliced
- 2 tablespoons chopped red onion
- 2 tablespoons fresh lemon juice
- 1 tablespoon apple cider vinegar
- 2 tablespoons Bragg's liquid aminos
- 3 tablespoons homemade mustard
- ½ cup vegetable broth
- 1 cup chopped chard
- Pinch of red pepper flakes
- Pinch of salt & pepper

Directions:

Sauté shrimp, garlic, onion, vinegar, Bragg's lemon juice and mustard until cooked through; transfer shrimp to a plate and deglaze pan with broth. Stir in chard and cook, stirring, until chard is tender. Serve chard sauce topped with shrimp.

Phase 3 modifications: Sauté with walnut, sesame or olive oil and serve topped with two tablespoons of roasted almonds.

Nutritional Information per Serving:

Calories: 217; Total Fat: 6 g; Carbs: 10.1 g; Dietary Fiber: 2.9 g; Sugars: 3.1 g; Protein: 29.1 g; Cholesterol: 211 mg; Sodium: 711 mg

Baked Fish w/ Asparagus

Yield: 1 Serving
Total Time: 30 Minutes
Prep Time: 10 Minutes
Cook Time: 20 Minutes

Ingredients

- 100 grams white fish
- ½ red onion, minced
- 1 clove garlic, minced
- 3 stalks asparagus
- 4 tablespoons fresh lemon juice
- 2 tablespoons caper juice
- ½ cup vegetable broth
- Bread crumbs
- Parsley
- ¼ teaspoon dried dill
- Pinch of tarragon
- Pinch of salt & pepper

Directions:

Layer asparagus and fish in a baking dish; mix spices and broth and add to the baking dish. Sprinkle with crumbs and bake at 350°F for about 20 minutes or until fish is cooked through.

Serve topped with cooking sauce, parsley and garnsihed with elmon wedges.

Nutritional Information per Serving:

Calories: 125; Total Fat: 2 g; Carbs: 15.3 g; Dietary Fiber: 1.3 g; Sugars: 3 g; Protein: 21.4 g; Cholesterol: 0 mg; Sodium: 565 mg

Citrus Orange Roughy BBQ Wrap

Yield: 1 Serving
Total Time: 25 Minutes
Prep Time: 10 Minutes
Cook Time: 15 Minutes

Ingredients

- 100 grams orange roughy fish
- 1 tablespoon chopped green onion
- 1 tablespoon fresh lemon juice
- 3 tablespoons fresh orange juice
- 3 orange slices
- Pinch of stevia
- Dash of onion powder
- Dash of garlic powder
- Pinch of salt & pepper

Directions:

Put fish in foil and baste with lemon juice and spices; top with lemon or orange slices and bake at 350°F for about 10-15 minutes or until fish is cooked through. Serve topped with juices and garnished with orange slices and parsley.

Nutritional Information per Serving:

Calories: 296; Total Fat: 1.6 g; Carbs: 52.3 g; Dietary Fiber: 9.8 g; Sugars: 41.3 g; Protein: 22.9 g; Cholesterol: 49 mg; Sodium: 40 mg

Poached Fish with Thyme

Yield: 1 Serving
Total Time: 15 Minutes
Prep Time: 10 Minutes
Cook Time: 5 Minutes

Ingredients

- 100 grams white fish
- ½ red onion, minced
- 1 clove garlic, minced
- 1 teaspoon apple cider vinegar
- ½ cup vegetable broth
- 2 tablespoons fresh lemon juice
- 2 tablespoons fresh caper juice
- Pinch of thyme
- Pinch of salt & pepper

Directions:

Mix liquid ingredients, onion and garlic; stir in fish and cook for about 5 minutes or until fish is cooked through. Serve garnished with lemon and parsley.

Phase 3 modifications: Drizzle fish with olive oil or melted butter. Serve topped with one tablespoon of capers.

Nutritional Information per Serving:

Calories: 185; Total Fat: 2 g; Carbs: 7.2 g; Dietary Fiber: 2.4 g; Sugars: 3.4 g; Protein: 23.8 g; Cholesterol: 55 mg; Sodium: 428 mg

Hot & Sweet Orange Shrimp

Yield: 1 Serving

Total Time: 25 Minutes

Prep Time: 10 Minutes

Cook Time: 15 Minutes

Ingredients

- 100 grams shrimp
- 1 serving sweet orange marinade
- ½ red onion, minced
- Pinch of stevia

Directions:

Marinate shrimp for at least 30 minutes; transfer to a frying pan along with marinade and add orange slices and pepper; sauté shrimp, deglazing pan with water, until cooked through.

Nutritional Information per Serving:

Calories: 223; Total Fat: 2.4 g; Carbs: 7.5 g; Dietary Fiber: 2.4 g; Sugars: 4.1 g; Protein: 22.9 g; Cholesterol: 211 mg; Sodium: 344 mg

Lobster in Tomato Sauce

Yield: 1 Serving
Total Time: 35 Minutes
Prep Time: 10 Minutes
Cook Time: 25 Minutes

Ingredients

- 100 grams raw lobster tail
- ½ red onion, minced
- 1 clove of garlic, minced
- 2 tablespoons fresh lemon juice
- 8 ounces tomato sauce
- 2 tomatoes, chopped
- Chopped parsley
- Pinch of cayenne pepper
- 1/8 teaspoon chopped tarragon
- 1/8 teaspoon thyme
- 1 bay leaf
- Pinch of salt & pepper

Directions:

Sauté lobster in juice and a splash of water; stir in onion, garlic, spices, tomato, and tomato sauce. Simmer for about 10-15 minutes. Serve immediately.

Phase 3 modifications: For a richer sauce, add a dollop of olive oil or butter and a splash of sherry or white wine and one tablespoon heavy cream.

Nutritional Information per Serving:

Calories: 201; Total Fat: 2 g; Carbs: 23.7 g; Dietary Fiber: 6.8 g; Sugars: 17.2 g; Protein: 24.6 g; Cholesterol: 146 mg; Sodium: 1693 mg

Baked Stuffed Lobster

Yield: 1 Serving
Total Time: 30 Minutes
Prep Time: 10 Minutes
Cook Time: 20 Minutes

Ingredients

- 100 grams raw lobster tail
- 1 clove garlic, minced
- ½ red onion, minced
- ½ cup vegetable broth
- Bread crumbs
- Pinch of paprika
- 1/8 teaspoon onion powder
- 1/8 teaspoon garlic powder
- Pinch of salt & pepper

Directions:

Mix onion, garlic, spices and crumbs; stuff lobster with mixture and place in a baking dish; add broth and sprinkle with paprika. Bake at 350°F for about 20 minutes and broil for about 2 minutes to brown. Season with salt and pepper and serve garnished with lemon wedges.

Phase 3 modifications: Add parmesan to the stuffing mixture and serve with melted butter.

Nutritional Information per Serving:

Calories: 182; Total Fat: 2.4 g; Carbs: 14.7 g; Dietary Fiber: 1 g; Sugars: 2.1 g; Protein: 23.6 g; Cholesterol: 146 mg; Sodium: 1039 mg

Savory Red Onion Caramelized Shrimp

Yield: 1 Serving
Total Time: 25 Minutes
Prep Time: 10 Minutes
Cook Time: 15 Minutes

Ingredients

- 100 grams shrimp
- 1 red onion, sliced into rings
- Vanilla flavored liquid stevia
- 1 tablespoons Bragg's liquid aminos
- 3 tablespoons fresh lemon juice
- ¼ cup water
- Pinch of salt & pepper

Directions:

Heat liquid ingredients in a pan over high heat and stir in shrimp, onion, pepper and salt; cook, until shrimp is cooked through.

Nutritional Information per Serving:

Calories: 174; Total Fat: 2.2 g; Carbs: 12.8 g; Dietary Fiber: 2.6 g; Sugars: 5.6 g; Protein: 24.4 g; Cholesterol: 211 mg; Sodium: 259 mg

Orange Roughy with Red Onion & Tomatoes

Yield: 1 Serving
Total Time: 20 Minutes
Prep Time: 10 Minutes
Cook Time: 10 Minutes

Ingredients

- 100 grams orange roughy fish
- 1 clove garlic, minced
- 2 tablespoons onion red chopped
- 2 tomatoes, chopped
- ½ cup vegetable broth
- Pinch of salt & pepper

Directions:

Sauté garlic and onions in broth; stir in spices and fish and cook for about 5 minutes. Add tomatoes and cook for 5 minutes more. Serve immediately sprinkled with salt and pepper and garnished with parsley.

Phase 3 modifications: Sauté garlic and onion in butter and add ¼ cup of half and half.

Nutritional Information per Serving:

Calories: 154; Total Fat: 2.1 g; Carbs: 12 g; Dietary Fiber: 3.4 g; Sugars: 7.7 g; Protein: 23.4 g; Cholesterol: 49 mg; Sodium: 430 mg

Sautéed Snapper with Hot Lemony Sauce

Yield: 1 Serving
Total Time: 20 Minutes
Prep Time: 10 Minutes
Cook Time: 10 Minutes

Ingredients

- 100 grams red snapper
- 2 tablespoons fresh caper juice
- 2 tablespoons fresh lemon juice
- ¼ cup vegetable broth
- Dash of cayenne
- Dash of onion powder
- Dash of garlic powder
- Pinch of salt & pepper

Directions:

Mix liquid ingredients with spices and add fish; cook for about 5-10 minutes and serve.

Phase 3 modifications: Add a tablespoon unsalted butter.

Nutritional Information per Serving:

Calories: 148; Total Fat: 2.3 g; Carbs: 1.5 g; Dietary Fiber: 0.2 g; Sugars: 1 g; Protein: 27.9 g; Cholesterol: 47 mg; Sodium: 254 mg

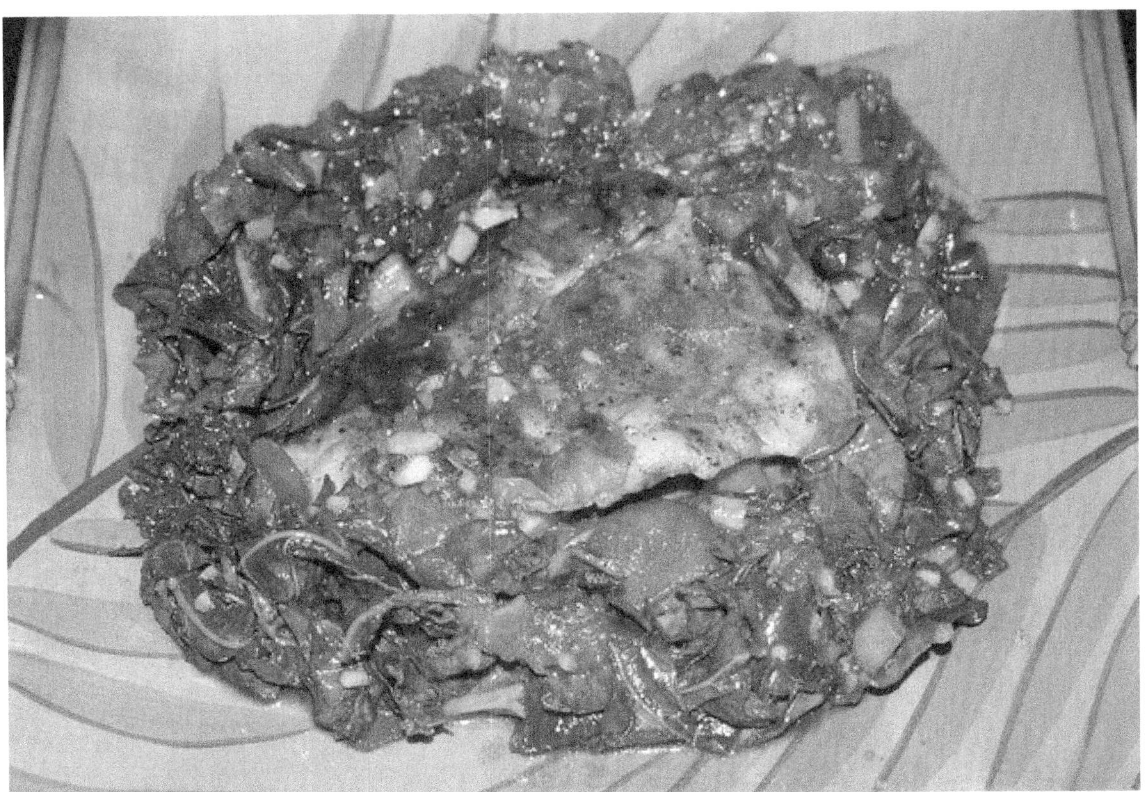

Delicious Red Snapper

Yield: 1 Serving
Total Time: 25 Minutes
Prep Time: 10 Minutes
Cook Time: 15 Minutes

Ingredients

- 100 grams red snapper fish
- ½ teaspoon nutmeg powder
- ½ teaspoon cumin
- 2 teaspoons oregano
- 1 teaspoon cayenne pepper
- 2 teaspoons garlic powder
- 2 teaspoons onion powder
- 4 teaspoons thyme
- 2 teaspoons paprika
- Blackening spice mix
- Pinch of stevia
- 2 teaspoons black pepper
- 2 teaspoons salt

Directions:

Mix spices and coat fish with the mixture; add fish to a preheated skillet and cook until fish is cooked through. Serve hot garnished with parsley and lemon.

Nutritional Information per Serving:

Calories: 216; Total Fat: 2.4 g; Carbs: 19 g; Dietary Fiber: 6.9 g; Sugars: 3.9 g; Protein: 29.9 g; Cholesterol: 47 mg; Sodium: 4720 mg

Baked Lobster w/ Spiced Lemon Sauce

Yield: 1 Serving
Total Time: 25 Minutes
Prep Time: 10 Minutes
Cook Time: 15 Minutes

Ingredients

- 100 grams sliced lobster tail
- 4 tablespoons lemon juice
- ¼ cup water
- Bread crumbs
- 1 teaspoon parsley
- Pinch of lemon zest
- Pinch of sweet paprika
- ¼ teaspoon garlic powder
- Pinch of red pepper flakes
- Pinch of salt & pepper

Directions:

Mix lemon juice, water and spices and bring to a boil; lower heat and cook until liquid is reduced. Place lobster in a baking dish and add lemon sauce; sprinkle with crumbs, salt pepper and paprika. Bake at 350°F for about 15 minutes or until lobster is cooked through. Serve lobster topped with sauce and garnished with lemon and parsley.

Nutritional Information per Serving:

Calories: 175; Total Fat: 2.2 g; Carbs: 4.9 g; Dietary Fiber: 1.2 g; Sugars: 2.6 g; Protein: 21.7 g; Cholesterol: 146 mg; Sodium: 671 mg

Mahi Mahi with Oranges

Yield: 1 Serving
Total Time: 35 Minutes
Prep Time: 10 Minutes
Cook Time: 25 Minutes

Ingredients

- 100 grams mahi mahi fish
- 1 clove garlic, minced
- 1 tablespoon chopped green onion
- 1 teaspoon apple cider vinegar
- 2 tablespoons Bragg's amino acids
- ½ orange in segments, chopped
- Pinch of stevia
- 1/8 teaspoon dried ginger
- Pinch of red pepper flakes
- Pinch of cayenne
- Water

Directions:

Sauté fish with Bragg's, vinegar, and a splash of water; add spices, garlic and stevia and chopped orange and cook for about 5-10 minutes. Serve over a bed of greens topped with green onion.

Nutritional Information per Serving:

Calories: 147; Total Fat: 1.1 g; Carbs: 13.7 g; Dietary Fiber: 2.5 g; Sugars: 8.8 g; Protein: 19.9 g; Cholesterol: 71 mg; Sodium: 99 mg

HCG Diet Vegetarian Meals

Yield: 1 Serving
Total Time: 13 Minutes
Prep Time: 10 Minutes
Cook Time: 3 Minutes

Tasty Greens

Ingredients

- 3 ounces greens
- ¾ cup water
- 1 ½ teaspoon Bragg's liquid aminos

Directions:

Combine greens and water in a medium pot; steam for about 2-3 minutes. Drain and serve the greens topped with aminos. Enjoy!

Nutritional Information per Serving:

Calories: 45; Total Fat: 0.9 g; Carbs: 4.2 g; Dietary Fiber: 2.7 g; Sugars: 0.3 g; Protein: 0.8 g; Cholesterol: 0 mg; Sodium: 321 mg

Zesty Asparagus

Yield: 1 Serving
Total Time: 10 Minutes
Prep Time: 5 Minutes
Cook Time: 5 Minutes

Ingredients

- 1/3 pound Asparagus, rinsed and cut diagonally into 1-inch pieces
- 4 tablespoons fresh lemon juice
- ¼ teaspoon Cayenne
- Pinch of salt & pepper
- 6 cups Water

Directions:

In a medium pot, bring water to a rolling boil; add asparagus and lower heat. Simmer for about 2 minutes and drain.

In a bowl, whisk together fresh lemon juice, cayenne, salt and pepper; toss in asparagus and serve.

Nutritional Information per Serving:

Calories: 37; Total Fat: 1.7 g; Carbs: 3.7 g; Dietary Fiber: 1.2 g; Sugars: 1.3 g; Protein: 0.1 g; Cholesterol: 0 mg; Sodium: 211 mg

Yield: 1 Serving
Total Time: 20 Minutes
Prep Time: 10 Minutes
Cook Time: 10 Minutes

Apple Cabbage

Ingredients

- 2 cups chopped cabbage
- 1 large apple, chopped
- 2 tablespoons Bragg's liquid aminos
- ¼ cup water
- ½ cup Bragg's apple cider vinegar
- 1 teaspoon onion powder
- 1 teaspoon garlic powder
- Pinch of salt & pepper

Directions:

In a nonstick skillet, sauté all the ingredients until apples and cabbage are tender. Serve right away!

Nutritional Information per Serving:

Calories: 112; Total Fat: 1.1 g; Carbs: 13.4 g; Dietary Fiber: 4.3 g; Sugars: 6.6 g; Protein: 2.1 g; Cholesterol: 20 mg; Sodium: 541 mg

Spiced Cucumbers

Yield: 2 Servings
Total Time: 5 Minutes
Prep Time: 5 Minutes
Cook Time: N/A

Ingredients

- 2 cups Cucumbers, Sliced
- 1/8 teaspoon Tony Chachere's Creole Seasoning

Directions:

In a large bowl, mix together all ingredients. Serve.

Variation: add cooked chicken.

Nutritional Information per Serving:

Calories: 29; Total Fat: 0.2 g; Carbs: 3.1 g; Dietary Fiber: 2.7 g; Sugars: 0 g; Protein: 0.1 g; Cholesterol: 0 mg; Sodium: 71 mg

Baked Vidalia Onion

Yield: 1 Serving
Total Time: 70 Minutes
Prep Time: 10 Minutes
Cook Time: 60 Minutes

Ingredients

- 1 medium Vidalia Onion
- Pinch of salt & pepper

Directions:

Preheat oven to 350°F.

Rinse onion and remove the outside, top and root; wrap in an aluminum foil and bake for about 60 minutes; season with salt and pepper.

Nutritional Information per Serving:

Calories: 11; Total Fat: 0 g; Carbs: 0 g; Dietary Fiber: 0 g; Sugars: 0 g; Protein: 0.1 g; Cholesterol: 0 mg; Sodium: 78 mg

Pico De Gallo

Yield: 1 Serving
Total Time: 10 Minutes
Prep Time: 10 Minutes
Cook Time: N/A

Ingredients

- 1 medium tomato, diced
- ½ onion, chopped
- 5 sprigs cilantro, chopped
- 4 rounds melba toast

Directions:

In a bowl, mix onion, tomato and cilantro and let sit for about 30-60 minutes. Scoop mixture with Melba toast.

Nutritional Information per Serving:

Calories: 192; Total Fat: 1.7 g; Carbs: 17.1 g; Dietary Fiber: 5.1 g; Sugars: 7.8 g; Protein: 2.4 g; Cholesterol: 0 mg; Sodium: 29 mg

Yield: 4 Servings
Total Time: 18 Minutes
Prep Time: 10 Minutes
Cook Time: 8 Minutes

Mediterranean Greens

Ingredients

- 6 ounces Greens
- 6 ounces Onions, Sliced
- ½ teaspoon all spice
- 2 tablespoons fresh lemon juice
- Pinch of salt & pepper

Directions:

Combine greens and water in a medium pot; steam for about 2-3 minutes and set aside.

Season onions with salt, all spice and pepper and then grill for about 5 minutes; mix with greens and lemon juice. Serve right away!

Nutritional Information per Serving:

Calories: 39; Total Fat: 1.4 g; Carbs: 5.1 g; Dietary Fiber: 3.4 g; Sugars: 1.2 g; Protein: 3.4 g; Cholesterol: 0 mg; Sodium: 91 mg

Citrus Tomato Salsa

Yield: 1 Serving
Total Time: 10 Minutes
Prep Time: 10 Minutes
Cook Time: N/A

Ingredients

- 1 large tomato, chopped
- 1 tablespoon fresh lemon juice
- 1/8 teaspoon celery salt
- 1/8 teaspoon chile powder
- 3 drops stevia
- 1 teaspoon cilantro

Directions:

Combine all the ingredients in a large bowl; refrigerate for about 1 hour or until chilled before serving.

Nutritional Information per Serving:

Calories: 52; Total Fat: 1.3 g; Carbs: 5.6 g; Dietary Fiber: 2.1 g; Sugars: 0.7 g; Protein: 1.4 g; Cholesterol: 0 mg; Sodium: 342 mg

Sautéed Cabbage

Yield: 1 Serving
Total Time: 25 Minutes
Prep Time: 10 Minutes
Cook Time: 15 Minutes

Ingredients

- 1 head red cabbage, finely chopped
- 1 clove garlic, minced
- ½ red onion, minced
- Fresh chopped cilantro
- Dash of cumin
- ¼ teaspoon cayenne pepper
- ¼ teaspoon Mexican oregano
- 1 cup vegetable broth
- Pinch of salt & pepper

Directions:

Sauté cabbage in liquid ingredients and a splash of water; stir in spices and cook until cabbage is tender; add ground chicken or beef if desired.

Nutritional Information per Serving:

Calories: 223; Total Fat: 2.3 g; Carbs: 45.9 g; Dietary Fiber: 18.7 g; Sugars: 24.5 g; Protein: 14.6 g; Cholesterol: 0 mg; Sodium: 1049 mg

Red Onion & Garlic Spiced Chard

Yield: 1 Serving
Total Time: 15 Minutes
Prep Time: 10 Minutes
Cook Time: 5 Minutes

Ingredients

- 4-6 cups Swiss chard
- ½ cup vegetable broth
- 1 tablespoon pure apple cider vinegar
- 4 tablespoons fresh lemon juice
- 6 cloves garlic, chopped
- 2 tablespoons chopped red onion
- ½ teaspoon garlic powder
- Pinch of salt & pepper

Directions:

Sauté garlic, onion, chard, spices in water and liquid ingredients for about 5 minutes. Serve sprinkled with lemon, salt and pepper.

Nutritional Information per Serving:

Calories: 217; Total Fat: 2.1 g; Carbs: 44.3 g; Dietary Fiber: 17.9 g; Sugars: 23.2 g; Protein: 13.2 g; Cholesterol: 0 mg; Sodium: 1021 mg

Baked Spiced Red Onion Garnish

Yield: 4 Servings
Total Time: 20 Minutes
Prep Time: 10 Minutes
Cook Time: 10 Minutes

Ingredients

- ½ red onion, thinly sliced into rings
- 1 clove garlic, minced
- 2 tablespoons fresh lemon juice
- ¼ cup pure apple cider vinegar
- 1 bay leaf
- Pinch of dried basil
- Pinch of oregano
- Pinch of salt & pepper
- Splash of water

Directions:

In a baking dish, combine onion, spices, water, and vinegar; bake at 350°F for about 10 minutes. Serve the sauce hot over chicken or beef or chilled over salads.

Phase 3 modifications: Brush onion with olive oil and bake or sauté in butter and spices; serve topped with Romano or parmesan cheese.

Nutritional Information per Serving:

Calories: 42; Total Fat: 0.8 g; Carbs: 11.9 g; Dietary Fiber: 2.8 g; Sugars: 3.1 g; Protein: 1.7 g; Cholesterol: 0 mg; Sodium: 53 mg

Radish Relish

Yield: 1-2 Servings
Total Time: 10 Minutes
Prep Time: 10 Minutes
Cook Time: N/A

Ingredients

- 7 red radishes
- 3 tablespoons apple cider vinegar
- Dash of onion powder
- Dash of garlic powder
- Pinch of salt & pepper
- Stevia

Directions:

Stir together spices; add radishes and marinate for at least 1 hour. Serve as a side dish or a topping on a protein.

Nutritional Information per Serving:

Calories: 17; Total Fat: 0 g; Carbs: 2 g; Dietary Fiber: 0.6 g; Sugars: 1 g; Protein: 0.3 g; Cholesterol: 0 mg; Sodium: 15 mg

Indian Spiced Spinach

Yield: 1-2 Servings
Total Time: 25 Minutes
Prep Time: 10 Minutes
Cook Time: 15 Minutes

Ingredients

- 1 cup chopped spinach
- ½ red onion, minced
- ¼ cup chicken broth
- 1/8 teaspoon turmeric
- Pinch of fresh grated ginger
- Pinch of ground coriander
- 1/8 teaspoon paprika
- 1/8 teaspoon cumin
- Pinch of salt & pepper

Directions:

Sauté onion and spices in broth; add spinach and cook until wilted. Serve.

Variations: add shrimp or chicken.

Phase 3 modifications: Add ghee or butter; stir in paneer cheese.

Nutritional Information per Serving:

Calories: 28; Total Fat: 0.6 g; Carbs: 3.9 g; Dietary Fiber: 1.3 g; Sugars: 1.2 g; Protein: 2.4 g; Cholesterol: 0 mg; Sodium: 216 mg

Grilled Asparagus w/ Lemony Rosemary Sauce

Yield: 1-2 Servings
Total Time: 20 Minutes
Prep Time: 10 Minutes
Cook Time: 10 Minutes

Ingredients

- 1 cup chopped asparagus
- 1 clove garlic, minced
- 1 tablespoon Bragg's liquid aminos
- 2 tablespoons fresh lemon juice
- Pinch of cayenne pepper
- Pinch of salt & pepper
- Dash of onion powder
- Dash of garlic powder
- ¼ teaspoon rosemary

Directions:

Marinate asparagus in Bragg's, garlic, lemon juice, cayenne pepper and salt; grill until tender.

Cook remaining marinade in a pan with spices, lemon rind and ½ cup water until pulp comes out and liquid is reduced by half. Discard rind and pour sauce over asparagus. Serve garnished with lemon and seasoned with salt and pepper.

Nutritional Information per Serving:

Calories: 38; Total Fat: 0.9 g; Carbs: 3.4 g; Dietary Fiber: 2.1 g; Sugars: 0.7 g; Protein: 1.1 g; Cholesterol: 0 mg; Sodium: 217 mg

Pickled Beet Greens

Yield: 1-2 Servings
Total Time: 20 Minutes
Prep Time: 10 Minutes
Cook Time: 10 Minutes

Ingredients

- 1 cup chopped beet greens
- ½ red onion, minced
- ¼ cup apple cider vinegar
- 1 tablespoon fresh lemon juice
- 1 tablespoon Bragg's amino acids
- 1 clove garlic, sliced
- ¼ teaspoon red pepper flakes
- Pinch of salt & pepper
- Stevia

Directions:

Mix spices and liquid ingredients; pour over beets and cook for about 5-10 minutes. Serve hot.

Phase 3 modifications1 cup: Add two tablespoons crumbled bacon.

Nutritional Information per Serving:

Calories: 69; Total Fat: 0.5 g; Carbs: 11.9 g; Dietary Fiber: 4.9 g; Sugars: 2.4 g; Protein: 4.3 g; Cholesterol: 0 mg; Sodium: 355 mg

Hot Pickled Cabbage

Yield: 1 Serving
Total Time: 1 Hour 10 Minutes
Prep Time: 10 Minutes
Cook Time: 1 Hour

Ingredients

- 1 cup chopped red cabbage
- 1 clove garlic, minced
- 2 tablespoons chopped red onion
- 2 tablespoons Bragg's liquid aminos
- ½ cup apple cider vinegar
- 1 apple, diced
- ¼ cup water
- Pinch of red pepper flakes
- Pinch of salt & pepper

Directions:

Slow cook apples and cabbage in vinegar and water until tender; stir in garlic, onion, spices, stevia, salt and pepper and serve hot.

Nutritional Information per Serving:

Calories: 25; Total Fat: 1 g; Carbs: 3.2 g; Dietary Fiber: 2.3 g; Sugars: 0.8 g; Protein: 1.1 g; Cholesterol: 0 mg; Sodium: 216 mg

Hot Peppered Chicory

Yield: 1-2 Servings
Total Time: 15 Minutes
Prep Time: 10 Minutes
Cook Time: 5 Minutes

Ingredients

- Chicory, minced
- ¼ cup vegetable broth
- 2 tablespoons fresh lemon juice
- Pinch of salt & pepper

Directions:

Mix chicory, lemon juice, broth, salt and pepper and cook for about 3-5 minutes. Serve hot.

Phase 3 modifications: Replace lemon juice with butter or olive oil; stir in cream cheese or half and half. Serve topped with feta or grated parmesan.

Nutritional Information per Serving:

Calories: 13; Total Fat: 0.1 g; Carbs: 1.2 g; Dietary Fiber: 0.7 g; Sugars: 0 g; Protein: 0.2 g; Cholesterol: 0 mg; Sodium: 121 mg

Roasted Tomato w/ Red Onion

Yield: 1-2 Servings
Total Time: 25 Minutes
Prep Time: 10 Minutes
Cook Time: 15 Minutes

Ingredients

- 1 red onion, sliced
- 1-2 cloves garlic, chopped
- 1 tomato, sliced
- Sprinkle of dried oregano
- 2 leaves fresh basil, chopped
- Squeeze of lemon juice
- Stevia
- Pinch of salt & pepper

Directions:

In a baking dish, lay out onion rings and sprinkle with lemon juice, salt and pepper; top with garlic, basil and tomato slices and bake at 375°F for about 10-15 minutes. Serve seasoned with lemon juice, salt and pepper.

Nutritional Information per Serving:

Calories: 23; Total Fat: 0.3 g; Carbs: 2.7 g; Dietary Fiber: 1.5 g; Sugars: 0.9 g; Protein: 1.1 g; Cholesterol: 0 mg; Sodium: 216 mg

HCG Diet Salads

Tasty Japanese Cucumber Salad

Yield: 1 Serving
Total Time: 10 Minutes
Prep Time: 10 Minutes
Cook Time: N/A

Ingredients

- ¼ red onion, minced
- 1 cup chopped cucumber
- 1 tablespoon Bragg's amino acids
- 1 tablespoon fresh lemon juice
- 2 tablespoon apple cider vinegar
- Stevia
- Cayenne pepper

Directions:

Combine all the ingredients together and marinate for about 15 minutes. Serve chilled.

Nutritional Information per Serving:

Calories: 27; Total Fat: 0.2 g; Carbs: 4.7 g; Dietary Fiber: 0.7 g; Sugars: 2.3 g; Protein: 0.8 g; Cholesterol: 0 mg; Sodium: 7 mg

Spiced Chicken Salad

Yield: 1 Serving
Total Time: 35 Minutes
Prep Time: 10 Minutes
Cook Time: 25 Minutes

Ingredients

- 1 apple, chopped
- ½ red onion, minced
- 2 tablespoons fresh lemon juice
- 1 clove garlic, minced
- 1/4 cup water
- Diced celery
- 100 grams diced chicken
- pinch of curry powder
- pinch of onion powder
- pinch of garlic powder
- pinch of turmeric
- pinch of cayenne pepper
- pinch of cinnamon
- stevia

Directions:

Sauté chicken in lemon juice until brown. Add spices and the ¼ cup water, stir well and simmer until sauce is formed and chicken well cooked. Add water and chill. Add celery and chopped apple. Serve.

Nutritional Information per Serving:

Calories: 288; Total Fat: 3.8 g; Carbs: 34.5 g; Dietary Fiber: 6.2 g; Sugars: 24.5 g; Protein: 30.3 g; Cholesterol: 77 mg; Sodium: 74 mg

Lobster Salad

Yield: 1 Serving
Total Time: 10 Minutes
Prep Time: 10 Minutes
Cook Time: N/A

Ingredients

- 100 grams diced lobster tail, cooked
- 1 cup chopped green onion
- 1 teaspoon apple cider vinegar
- 1 teaspoon fresh lemon juice
- Pinch of salt & pepper
- Tarragon
- Stevia
- Sliced steamed fennel bulb, tomatoes or celery

Directions:

Combine liquid ingredients, spices and lobster together and serve over arugula greens, salad or another vegetable

Mix lobster, liquid ingredients and spices together and serve over a salad, arugula greens, or with another vegetable.

Nutritional Information per Serving:

Calories: 124; Total Fat: 1.1 g; Carbs: 7.6 g; Dietary Fiber: 2.7 g; Sugars: 2.5 g; Protein: 20.9 g; Cholesterol: 46 mg; Sodium: 503 mg

Spicy Crab Salad

Yield: 1 Serving
Total Time: 20 Minutes
Prep Time: 10 Minutes
Cook Time: 10 Minutes

Ingredients

- 100 grams crab
- 2 teaspoons apple cider vinegar
- 1 tablespoon Bragg's liquid aminos
- ½ red onion, minced
- 1 tablespoon fresh lemon juice
- Pinch of cayenne pepper
- Pinch of onion powder
- Diced celery
- Pinch of garlic powder
- Pinch of salt & pepper

Directions:

Steam the crab and chop into medium sizes. Toss with spices, liquid ingredients and onions.

Marinate for at least 15 minutes. Serve over green salad or add diced celery.

Nutritional Information per Serving:

Calories: 112; Total Fat: 1.9 g; Carbs: 1.3 g; Dietary Fiber: 0.3 g; Sugars: 0.8 g; Protein: 20.4 g; Cholesterol: 100 mg; Sodium: 283 mg

Cabbage-Orange Salad w/ Chicken

Yield: 1 Serving
Total Time: 35 Minutes
Prep Time: 20 Minutes
Cook Time: 15 Minutes

Ingredients

- 100 grams chicken
- 1 tablespoon Bragg's liquid aminos
- 1 tablespoon apple cider vinegar
- 2 tablespoons lemon juice
- ½ head cabbage, chopped
- 3 tablespoons fresh orange juice
- 1 orange, sliced
- Pinch of cayenne
- Pinch of ginger powder
- Pinch of salt and pepper
- Stevia

Directions:

In lemon juice, apple cider vinegar and spices, marinate the chicken strips; cook and brown slightly. Prepare dressing with Bragg's, black pepper, 3 tablespoons of orange juice, stevia, cayenne, black pepper and salt. Shred the cabbage finely and mix with dressing. Marinate for about 20 minutes or more. Top with orange slices and chicken.

Phase 3 modifications: Drizzle with sesame or olive oil and serve topped with sesame seeds or sliced almonds.

Nutritional Information per Serving:

Calories: 360; Total Fat: 4 g; Carbs: 48.3 g; Dietary Fiber: 13.7 g; Sugars: 33.3 g; Protein: 35.9 g; Cholesterol: 77 mg; Sodium: 135 mg

Red Cabbage Salad

Yield: 1-2 Servings

Total Time: 10 Minutes

Prep Time: 10 Minutes

Cook Time: N/A

Ingredients

- ½ head red cabbage, chopped
- ¼ teaspoon onion powder
- 1 clove garlic, minced
- ¼ teaspoon garlic powder
- Pinch of cayenne pepper
- 3 tablespoon Bragg's liquid aminos
- 3 tablespoon fresh lemon juice
- Pinch of salt & pepper
- ¼ cup apple cider vinegar
- ½ red onion, minced
- Stevia

Directions:

Mix together liquid ingredients and spices. Coat the cabbage with dressing and marinate for at least 1 hour to mix flavors.

Phase 3 modifications: Add olive oil or flax seed oil. Toss with crumbled bacon or gorgonzola cheese.

Nutritional Information per Serving:

Calories: 127; Total Fat: 0.8 g; Carbs: 25.3 g; Dietary Fiber: 9.6 g; Sugars: 13.5 g; Protein: 5.5 g; Cholesterol: 0 mg; Sodium: 78 mg

Orange Cucumber Salad

Yield: 1 Serving
Total Time: 10 Minutes
Prep Time: 10 Minutes
Cook Time: N/A

Ingredients

- 1 cucumber, sliced
- 1 teaspoon apple cider vinegar
- ½ red onion, minced
- 1 teaspoon minced fresh tarragon
- 1 orange, sliced
- Chopped fresh mint leaves
- 1 tablespoon fresh lemon juice
- 2 tablespoons fresh orange juice
- Pinch of salt & pepper
- Stevia

Directions:

Mix together onion, stevia, spices and apple cider vinegar. Add orange slices, cucumber, salt, pepper and tarragon. Marinate for around 30 minutes and serve garnished with chopped mint.

Phase 3 modifications: Drizzle salad with hazelnut and serve topped with toasted pine nuts.

Nutritional Information per Serving:

Calories: 156; Total Fat: 2.1 g; Carbs: 37.4 g; Dietary Fiber: 6.3 g; Sugars: 25.6 g; Protein: 4.3 g; Cholesterol: 0 mg; Sodium: 0 mg

Yield: 1 Serving
Total Time: 10 Minutes
Prep Time: 10 Minutes
Cook Time: N/A

Fennel Citrus Salad

Ingredients

- 3 fennel bulbs, steamed
- 2 tablespoons fresh lemon juice
- 1 sliced orange or ½ diced grapefruit
- Stevia
- Chopped mint or cilantro

Directions:

Cut citrus into large slices and fennel bulb into thin slices. Mix all the ingredients together in a bowl and chill.

Phase 3 modifications: Add olive oil and serve topped with pine nuts

Nutritional Information per Serving:

Calories: 57; Total Fat: 0.1 g; Carbs: 8.3 g; Dietary Fiber: 4.7; Sugars: 1.8 g; Protein: 1.2 g; Cholesterol: 0 mg; Sodium: 13 mg

Spicy Thai-Style Cucumber Salad

Yield: 1-2 Servings
Total Time: 10 Minutes
Prep Time: 10 Minutes
Cook Time: N/A

Ingredients

- 1 rolled and sliced basil leaf
- 1 tablespoon chopped green onion
- 1 minced clove of garlic
- 2 tablespoons fresh lemon juice
- 2 tablespoons Bragg's liquid aminos
- 2 tablespoons vegetable broth
- 1 teaspoon chopped cilantro
- 1 whole cucumber, sliced into long strips
- 1/8 teaspoon red chili flakes
- Pinch of salt & pepper

Directions:

Combine all liquid ingredients with the fresh herbs, garlic, chili flakes and onion. Add cucumber strips and coat with the mixture of spices. Marinate for at least 10 minutes.

Phase 3 modifications: Add a little sesame oil or chili oil. Add chopped bell pepper or other vegetables. Top with a tablespoon of crushed peanuts.

Nutritional Information per Serving:

Calories: 71; Total Fat: 1.1 g; Carbs: 9.2 g; Dietary Fiber: 4.7; Sugars: 2.8 g; Protein: 1.7 g; Cholesterol: 0 mg; Sodium: 243 mg

Sweet & Crunchy Apple Chicken Salad

Yield: 1 Serving
Total Time: 10 Minutes
Prep Time: 10 Minutes
Cook Time: N/A

Ingredients

- Pinch of cardamom
- 1/8 teaspoon cinnamon
- 3 diced stalks celery
- Pinch of salt
- 1 diced apple
- Stevia
- 100 grams cooked chicken, diced
- 3 tablespoons fresh lemon juice
- Wedge of lemon
- Nutmeg

Directions:

Combine the ingredients and sprinkle with cinnamon and stevia. Cool for about 20 minutes. Serve with wedge of lemon.

Phase 3 modifications: Add chopped almonds or walnuts and mix in Greek yogurt or mayonnaise.

Nutritional Information per Serving:

Calories: 138; Total Fat: 0.9 g; Carbs: 34.2 g; Dietary Fiber: 6.8; Sugars: 25 g; Protein: 1.4 g; Cholesterol: 0 mg; Sodium: 207 mg

Curried Celery Salad

Yield: 1 Serving
Total Time: 10 Minutes
Prep Time: 10 Minutes
Cook Time: N/A

Ingredients

- 1 tablespoon apple cider vinegar
- 2 tablespoons Bragg's liquid aminos
- 1 teaspoon curry powder
- 1 tablespoon chopped green onions
- 3 tablespoons fresh lemon juice
- Diced celery stalks diced
- Stevia

Directions:

Mix thoroughly all liquid ingredients and spices. Coat the celery and marinate the flavors for 20 to 30 minutes. Serve.

Variations: Add diced tomatoes.

Nutritional Information per Serving:

Calories: 26; Total Fat: 0.3 g; Carbs: 3.2 g; Dietary Fiber: 1.7; Sugars: 0.8 g; Protein: 0.7 g; Cholesterol: 0 mg; Sodium: 165 mg

Strawberry & Cucumber Salad

Yield: 1 Serving
Total Time: 10 Minutes
Prep Time: 10 Minutes
Cook Time: N/A

Ingredients

- Fresh ground white pepper
- 8 strawberries, sliced
- 1 cucumber, sliced
- Stevia
- 1 serving strawberry vinaigrette

Directions:

In a large bowl, mix all ingredients and marinate for at least 10 minutes.

Nutritional Information per Serving:

Calories: 91; Total Fat: 0.8 g; Carbs: 22 g; Dietary Fiber: 4.4 g; Sugars: 12.1 g; Protein: 2.9 g; Cholesterol: 0 mg; Sodium: 7 mg

Chinese Chicken Salad

Yield: 1 Serving
Total Time: 25 Minutes
Prep Time: 10 Minutes
Cook Time: 15 Minutes

Ingredients

- 100 grams chicken breast
- 1 cup shredded cabbage
- 1 tablespoon minced green onion
- 1 clove of minced garlic
- 3 tablespoon Bragg's liquid aminos
- Pinch of red pepper flakes
- 1 tablespoon apple cider vinegar
- Powdered ginger or fresh grated ginger
- Pinch of salt & pepper
- Stevia

Directions:

Brown the chicken with onion, lemon juice, garlic and the Bragg's. Steam and drain excess moisture; add chicken, salt and pepper and ginger. Allow to chill. Sprinkle more Bragg's liquid aminos.

Phase 3 modifications: Add sesame oil and other veggies as bell peppers.

Nutritional Information per Serving:

Calories: 277; Total Fat: 3.1 g; Carbs: 30.1 g; Dietary Fiber: 7.7 g; Sugars: 17.4 g; Protein: 31.2 g; Cholesterol: 77 mg; Sodium: 242 mg

Apple & Asparagus Salad

Yield: 1 Serving
Total Time: 20 Minutes
Prep Time: 10 Minutes
Cook Time: 10 Minutes

Ingredients

- 1 apple, diced
- 8 stalks asparagus, chopped
- 1 red onion, minced
- 4 tablespoons fresh lemon juice
- ¼ teaspoon cinnamon or garam masala
- Stevia
- Water
- Pinch of salt & pepper

Directions:

Allow asparagus to marinate in vinaigrette for about 10 minutes. In lemon juice, sauté asparagus until cooked lightly. Mix with spices, onion and apple. Add stevia, salt and pepper. Refrigerate for about 10 minutes. Serve hot as a side dish or as a salad.

Nutritional Information per Serving:

Calories: 276; Total Fat: 3.2 g; Carbs: 32.3 g; Dietary Fiber: 6.3 g; Sugars: 24.4 g; Protein: 30.7 g; Cholesterol: 77 mg; Sodium: 223 mg

Arugula Salad w/ Fruit & Chicken

Yield: 1 Serving
Total Time: 25 Minutes
Prep Time: 10 Minutes
Cook Time: 15 Minutes

Ingredients

- 100 grams chicken
- 2 cups arugula
- Strawberry, apple, grapefruit or orange slices
- 1 tablespoon chopped red onion
- Pinch of salt & pepper
- Favorite dressing

Directions:

Brown the chicken in a little water and lemon juice. Prepare arugula and place sliced chicken on the arugula salad. Top with fruit and drizzle with dressing.

Nutritional Information per Serving:

Calories: 281; Total Fat: 3.7 g; Carbs: 33.2 g; Dietary Fiber: 6.3 g; Sugars: 24.4 g; Protein: 30.7 g; Cholesterol: 77 mg; Sodium: 231 mg

Chicken Salad w/ Celery

Yield: 1 Serving
Total Time: 20 Minutes
Prep Time: 10 Minutes
Cook Time: 10 Minutes

Ingredients

- 100 grams chicken
- 1 tablespoon fresh lemon juice
- 2 tablespoons Bragg's liquid aminos
- 1 teaspoon apple cider vinegar
- 1 red onion, minced
- Pinch of salt & pepper
- ¼ teaspoon poultry seasoning
- Celery

Directions:

Cook the chicken lightly in chicken broth or water. Chop all the ingredients finely. Add liquid ingredients and spices and mix thoroughly with diced celery. Serve.

Nutritional Information per Serving:

Calories: 191; Total Fat: 2.9 g; Carbs: 24.5 g; Dietary Fiber: 6.2 g; Sugars: 18.9 g; Protein: 32.3 g; Cholesterol: 77 mg; Sodium: 254 mg

Tasty Taco Salad

Yield: 1 Serving
Total Time: 20 Minutes
Prep Time: 5 Minutes
Cook Time: 15 Minutes

Ingredients

- 2 cups chopped romaine lettuce
- 3 ounces lean ground beef
- ¼ teaspoon garlic
- Pinch of salt
- ¼ teaspoon chili seasoning
- 1 crumbled melba toast

Directions:

Season beef and sauté; sprinkle over chopped lettuce and top with Melba toast crumbs. Serve.

Nutritional Information per Serving:

Calories: 176; Total Fat: 5.5 g; Carbs: 3.8 g; Dietary Fiber: 0.7 g; Sugars: 1.1 g; Protein: 26.4 g; Cholesterol: 76 mg; Sodium: 81 mg

Yield: 1 Serving
Total Time: 10 Minutes
Prep Time: 10 Minutes
Cook Time: N/A

Delicious Chicory Salad

Ingredients

- 1 cup chopped fresh chicory
- 1 tablespoon fresh lemon juice
- 1 tablespoon Bragg's liquid aminos
- 2 teaspoons apple cider vinegar
- Pinch of salt & pepper

Directions:

Mix chicory, lemon juice, vinegar, salt and pepper; serve right away.

Phase 2 variations: Add fresh mint and tomatoes or stir in a little orange juice. Add minced garlic and red onion or apple and stevia.

Phase 3 modifications: Add hazelnut, walnut or olive oil and serve sprinkled with feta and a tablespoon of walnuts.

Nutritional Information per Serving:

Calories: 217; Total Fat: 2.1 g; Carbs: 44.3 g; Dietary Fiber: 17.9 g; Sugars: 23.2 g; Protein: 13.2 g; Cholesterol: 0 mg; Sodium: 1021 mg

Chilled Tomato Salad

Yield: 1-2 Servings
Total Time: 10 Minutes
Prep Time: 10 Minutes
Cook Time: N/A

Ingredients

- 1 cup chopped tomatoes
- 1 garlic clove, minced
- 1 tablespoon green onion, chopped
- ¼ cup apple cider vinegar
- 1/8 teaspoon marjoram
- 1/8 teaspoon thyme
- ¼ teaspoon basil
- Dash of mustard powder
- Pinch of salt & pepper

Directions:

Mix spices and vinegar and pour over tomato; marinate for at least 1 hour and serve.

Phase 3 modifications: Stir in mayonnaise or olive oil and sliced green olives and Swiss or feta cheese.

Nutritional Information per Serving:

Calories: 67; Total Fat: 0.7 g; Carbs: 4.1 g; Dietary Fiber: 2.3 g; Sugars: 1.2 g; Protein: 1.1 g; Cholesterol: 0 mg; Sodium: 221 mg

HCG Diet Appetizers, Desserts & Snacks

Dreamy Fruit Cup

Yield: 1 Serving
Total Time: 5 Minutes
Prep Time: 5 Minutes
Cook Time: N/A

Ingredients

- ½ teaspoon Orange Rind
- 1/4 cup strawberry juice
- 1 cup Strawberries
- 1-2 drops Stevia
- 1 cup chopped Green Apple
- ½ cup fat-free Whip Topping

Directions:

In a food processor, blend together strawberries, orange rind and stevia until chunky.

Place ¼ cup strawberry mixture and ¼ cup apple; serve topped with whip topping. Enjoy!

Nutritional Information per Serving:

Calories: 209; Total Fat: 1.3 g; Carbs: 53.2 g; Dietary Fiber: 11.3 g; Sugars: 37.3 g; Protein: 2.6 g; Cholesterol: 0 mg; Sodium: 5 mg

Strawberry Sorbet

Yield: 1 Serving
Total Time: 5 Minutes
Prep Time: 5 Minutes
Cook Time: N/A

Ingredients

- 4-6 medium strawberries
- 2 tablespoons fresh lemon juice
- ½ teaspoon vanilla powder
- Flavored stevia
- Ice cubes
- ¼ cup water

Directions:

In a blender, blend all ingredients until very smooth; pour into molds and freeze until firm.

Phase 3 modifications: Add half and half or cream and whipped egg whites.

Nutritional Information per Serving:

Calories: 26; Total Fat: 0.3 g; Carbs: 4.7 g; Dietary Fiber: 2.7 g; Sugars: 1.7 g; Protein: 1.6 g; Cholesterol: 0 mg; Sodium: 9 mg

Lemon Pops

Yield: 1 Serving
Total Time: 5 Minutes
Prep Time: 5 Minutes
Cook Time: N/A

Ingredients

- 4 tablespoons fresh lemon juice
- Powdered stevia

Directions:

Mix orange or lemon juice and stevia and pour into molds; freeze until firm.

Nutritional Information per Serving:

Calories: 0; Total Fat: 0 g; Carbs: 0 g; Dietary Fiber: 0 g; Sugars: 0 g; Protein: 0g; Cholesterol: 0 mg; Sodium: 10 mg

Apple Chips

Yield: 1 Serving
Total Time: 25 Minutes
Prep Time: 10 Minutes
Cook Time: 15 Minutes

Ingredients

- 1 apple, sliced thinly
- Dash of cinnamon
- Stevia

Directions:

Coat apple slices with cinnamon and stevia and bake at 325°F for about 15 minutes or until tender and crispy.

Nutritional Information per Serving:

Calories: 146; Total Fat: 0.7 g; Carbs: 36.4 g; Dietary Fiber: 6.8 g; Sugars: 26.4 g; Protein: 1.6 g; Cholesterol: 0 mg; Sodium: 10 mg

Apple Cookies

Yield: 1 Serving
Total Time: 30 Minutes
Prep Time: 10 Minutes
Cook Time: 20 Minutes

Ingredients

- Pulp from 1 apple
- 1 tablespoon fresh lemon juice
- 1/8 teaspoon vanilla powder
- Pinch of nutmeg
- 1/8 teaspoon cinnamon
- Stevia

Directions:

Mix apple pulp, spices and stevia and form into two cookies; bake at 325°F for about 15-20 minutes or until browned.

Phase 3 modifications: Add a tablespoon butter and chopped pecans and walnuts to apple mixture before baking.

Nutritional Information per Serving:

Calories: 146; Total Fat: 0.7 g; Carbs: 36.4 g; Dietary Fiber: 6.8 g; Sugars: 26.4 g; Protein: 1.6 g; Cholesterol: 0 mg; Sodium: 10 mg

Spicy Frozen Orange Slices

Yield: 1 Serving
Total Time: 10 Minutes
Prep Time: 10 Minutes
Cook Time: N/A

Ingredients

- 2 tablespoons fresh lemon juice
- Pinch of cardamom
- Pinch of powdered clove
- Pinch of nutmeg
- ¼ teaspoon powdered vanilla
- ¼ teaspoon cinnamon
- Powdered stevia

Directions:

Mix spices and stevia; dip orange slices into lemon juice and then coat with spice mixture. Freeze until firm.

Variations: use apple slices or strawberries.

Nutritional Information per Serving:

Calories: 7; Total Fat: 0.1 g; Carbs: 1.3 g; Dietary Fiber: 0.6 g; Sugars: 0.4 g; Protein: 1.2 g; Cholesterol: 0 mg; Sodium: 10 mg

Apple Slices w/ Cinnamon Sauce

Yield: 1 Serving
Total Time: 15 Minutes
Prep Time: 10 Minutes
Cook Time: 5 Minutes

Ingredients

- 1 apple, sliced
- 1 teaspoon apple cider vinegar
- 3 tablespoons fresh lemon juice
- Dash of nutmeg
- 1-2 teaspoons cinnamon
- Powdered stevia

Directions:

Heat apple slices and liquid ingredients in a microwave, stirring, until thick. Serve with apple slices.

Phase 3 modifications: mix lemon juice and spices and whisk in butter add vanilla or rum.

Nutritional Information per Serving:

Calories: 144; Total Fat: 0.8 g; Carbs: 36.1 g; Dietary Fiber: 6.8 g; Sugars: 26.4 g; Protein: 1.6 g; Cholesterol: 0 mg; Sodium: 10 mg

Fruit with Vanilla Sauce

Yield: 1 Serving
Total Time: 10 Minutes
Prep Time: 10 Minutes
Cook Time: N/A

Ingredients

- 1 apple
- ½ teaspoon apple cider vinegar
- 2 tablespoons fresh lemon juice
- 1 tablespoon vanilla powder
- Powdered stevia

Directions:

Stir together lemon juice, vanilla powder and stevia; heat the sauce and pour into dipping bowl. Serve with fresh fruit.

Phase 3 modifications: Stir in a tablespoon butter until blended.

Nutritional Information per Serving:

Calories: 146; Total Fat: 0.7 g; Carbs: 36.4 g; Dietary Fiber: 6.8 g; Sugars: 26.4 g; Protein: 1.6 g; Cholesterol: 0 mg; Sodium: 10 mg

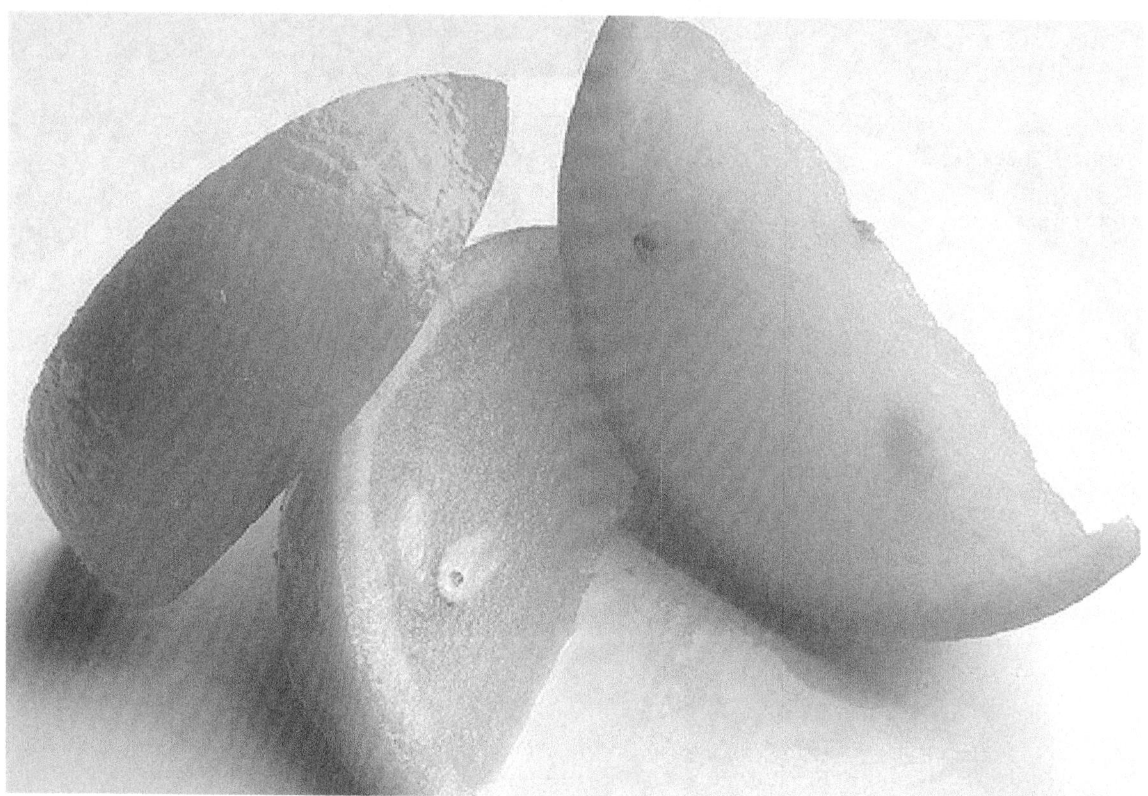

Warm Spicy Oranges

Yield: 1 Serving
Total Time: 18 Minutes
Prep Time: 10 Minutes
Cook Time: 8 Minutes

Ingredients

- 1 orange, segmented
- 2 tablespoons fresh lemon juice
- 1/8 teaspoon powdered vanilla
- 1/8 teaspoon ground cinnamon
- Dash of nutmeg
- Stevia
- Dash of cloves

Directions:

In a pan, mix lemon juice, spices and stevia and warm through; add oranges and cook for about 3 minutes. Serve hot.

Nutritional Information per Serving:

Calories: 11; Total Fat: 0.1 g; Carbs: 3.6 g; Dietary Fiber: 1.8 g; Sugars: 2.4 g; Protein: 1.7 g; Cholesterol: 0 mg; Sodium: 21 mg

Frozen Grapefruit Spears

Yield: 1 Serving
Total Time: 10 Minutes
Prep Time: 10 Minutes
Cook Time: N/A

Ingredients

- ½ grapefruit, segmented
- 2 tablespoons fresh lemon juice
- Powdered stevia
- Pinch of lemon zest

Directions:

Dip grapefruit into fresh lemon juice and coat with lemon zest and stevia; freeze until firm and serve.

Nutritional Information per Serving:

Calories: 46; Total Fat: 0.2 g; Carbs: 4.9 g; Dietary Fiber: 1.3 g; Sugars: 3.1 g; Protein: 1.3 g; Cholesterol: 0 mg; Sodium: 11 mg

Frozen Cocoa Strawberries

Yield: 1 Serving
Total Time: 10 Minutes
Prep Time: 10 Minutes
Cook Time: N/A

Ingredients

- 6 medium strawberries, sliced
- 1 tablespoon cocoa powder
- Powdered stevia

Directions:

Mix stevia and cocoa; dip sliced strawberries into the mixture and freeze until firm.

Variations: Use orange slices.

Nutritional Information per Serving:

Calories: 31; Total Fat: 0.2 g; Carbs: 7.1 g; Dietary Fiber: 1.8 g; Sugars: 5.2 g; Protein: 2.2 g; Cholesterol: 0 mg; Sodium: 17 mg

Warm Strawberry Compote

Yield: 1 Serving
Total Time: 25 Minutes
Prep Time: 10 Minutes
Cook Time: 15 Minutes

Ingredients

- 6 strawberries, sliced
- 2 tablespoons fresh lemon juice
- Dark chocolate stevia
- Dash of cayenne
- Dash of nutmeg
- Dash of cinnamon
- Dash of salt

Directions:

Combine all ingredients and sauté over medium heat until thick. Serve warm garnished with mint and topped with cinnamon Melba croutons.

Phase 3 modifications: Replace e lemon juice with two tablespoons of heavy cream or cream cheese; serve topped with roasted nuts.

Nutritional Information per Serving:

Calories: 33; Total Fat: 0.6 g; Carbs: 6.7 g; Dietary Fiber: 1.8 g; Sugars: 4.3 g; Protein: 0.8 g; Cholesterol: 0 mg; Sodium: 162 mg

Applesauce with Cinnamon

Yield: 1 Serving
Total Time: 10 Minutes
Prep Time: 10 Minutes
Cook Time: N/A

Ingredients

- 1 apple
- Powdered stevia
- ½ teaspoon cinnamon
- Pinch of nutmeg

Directions:

Puree apple in a food processor along with stevia and cinnamon.

Chill before serving.

Nutritional Information per Serving:

Calories: 146; Total Fat: 0.7 g; Carbs: 36.4 g; Dietary Fiber: 6.8 g; Sugars: 26.4 g; Protein: 1.6 g; Cholesterol: 0 mg; Sodium: 10 mg

Dark Chocolate Flavored Orange Slices

Yield: 1 Serving
Total Time: 10 Minutes
Prep Time: 10 Minutes
Cook Time: N/A

Ingredients

- 1 orange, peeled and sliced
- Dark chocolate stevia extract

Directions:

Place strawberry or orange slices in a bowl and drizzle with dark chocolate stevia. Chill and serve garnished with mint.

Nutritional Information per Serving:

Calories: 86; Total Fat: 0.2 g; Carbs: 21.6 g; Dietary Fiber: 4.4 g; Sugars: 17.2 g; Protein: 1.7 g; Cholesterol: 0 mg; Sodium: 0 mg

Healthy Apple Snack

Yield: 1 Serving
Total Time: 5 Minutes
Prep Time: 5 Minutes
Cook Time: N/A

Ingredients

- 1 apple, thinly sliced
- 1/3 packet Stevia
- Pinch of cinnamon Powder

Directions:

Place sliced apple in a serving bowl and sprinkle with stevia and cinnamon. Enjoy!

Nutritional Information per Serving:

Calories: 145; Total Fat: 0.7 g; Carbs: 36.4 g; Dietary Fiber: 6.8 g; Sugars: 26.4 g; Protein: 1.6 g; Cholesterol: 0 mg; Sodium: 10 mg

Tasty Fruity Salad

Yield: 4 Servings
Total Time: 5 Minutes
Prep Time: 5 Minutes
Cook Time: N/A

Ingredients

- 1 cup blueberries
- 1 cup diced pineapple
- 1 cup chopped banana
- 1 cup strawberries

Directions:

In a large bowl, mix all the ingredients and serve.

Nutritional Information per Serving:

Calories: 86; Total Fat: 0.4 g; Carbs: 22 g; Dietary Fiber: .2 g; Sugars: 14 g; Protein: 1.6 g; Cholesterol: 0 mg; Sodium: 1 mg

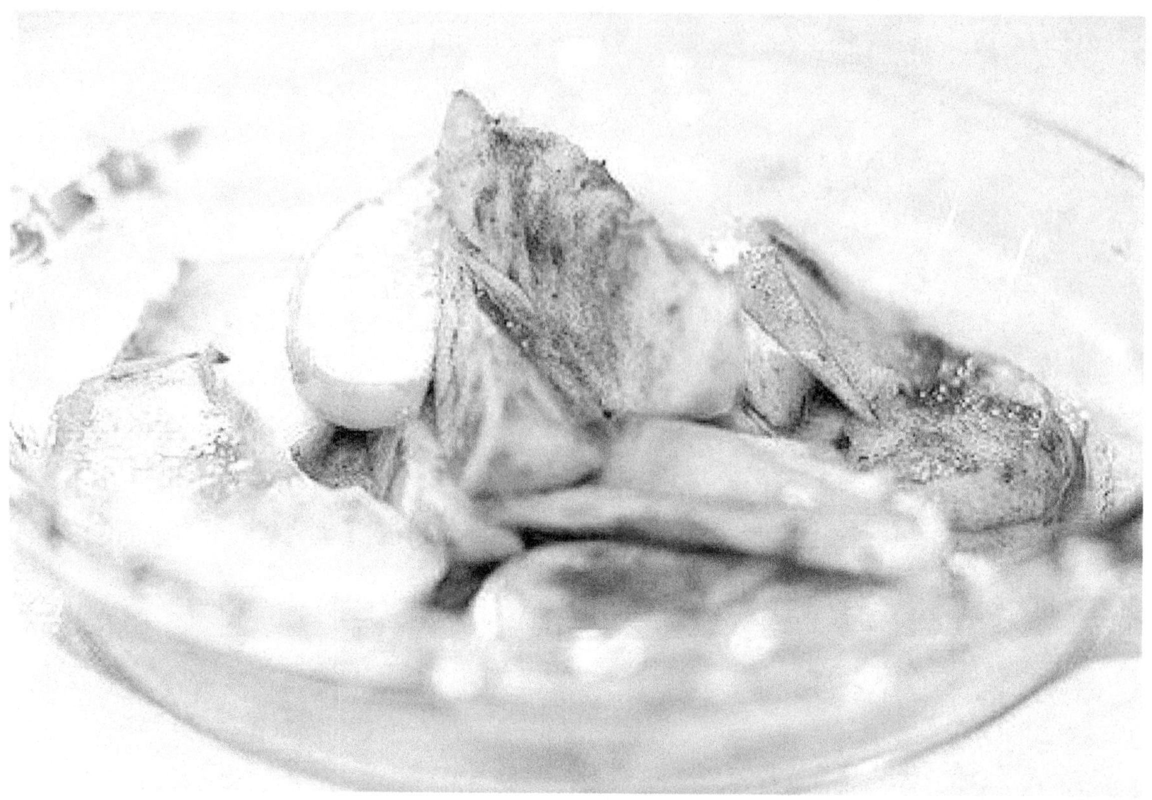

Apple Candy

Yield: 4 Servings
Total Time: 70 Minutes
Prep Time: 10 Minutes
Cook Time: 60 Minutes

Ingredients

- 4 apples
- 2 packets stevia
- 1 teaspoon cinnamon
- 1 teaspoon vanilla
- 2 cups water

Directions:

Add apples in a square baking dish.

Stir stevia in 2 tablespoons of water; pour over the apples and sprinkle with cinnamon and add the remaining water. Bake in a 350°F oven for about 50-60 minutes. Transfer the apples to a dish. Stir vanilla in the cooking liquid and pour over the apples. Serve warm.

Nutritional Information per Serving:

Calories: 143; Total Fat: 0.7 g; Carbs: 35.4 g; Dietary Fiber: 6.8 g; Sugars: 26.4 g; Protein: 1.6 g; Cholesterol: 0 mg; Sodium: 9 mg

Applesauce

Yield: 1 Serving
Total Time: 25 Minutes
Prep Time: 10 Minutes
Cook Time: 15 Minutes

Ingredients

- 1 large apple, chopped
- ¼ cup Water
- Dash of Cinnamon
- 1 packet Stevia

Directions:

In a small saucepan, mix apple, water and cinnamon; bring to a boil. Lower heat and stir in stevia; simmer, stirring occasionally, until water is evaporated. Remove the pan from heat and transfer the mixture to a food processor or blender; blend until smooth, adding water as needed.

Nutritional Information per Serving:

Calories: 142; Total Fat: 0.6 g; Carbs: 35.4 g; Dietary Fiber: 6.8 g; Sugars: 26.4 g; Protein: 1.6 g; Cholesterol: 0 mg; Sodium: 11 mg

Apple & Strawberry Snack

Yield: 1 Serving
Total Time: 7 Minutes
Prep Time: 5 Minutes
Cook Time: 2 Minutes

Ingredients

- ½ apple, cored and sliced
- 2-3 strawberries
- dash of ground cinnamon
- 2-3 drops stevia 2-3 drops

Directions:

In a bowl, mix strawberries and apples and sprinkle with stevia and cinnamon; microwave for about 1-2 minutes. Serve warm.

Nutritional Information per Serving:

Calories: 145; Total Fat: 0.8 g; Carbs: 34.2 g; Dietary Fiber: 7.8 g; Sugars: 24.4 g; Protein: 1.6 g; Cholesterol: 0 mg; Sodium: 11 mg

Shrimp Cocktail

Yield: 1 Serving

Total Time: 5 Minutes

Prep Time: 10 Minutes

Cook Time: 15 Minutes

Ingredients

- 100 grams steamed shrimp
- 1 tablespoon apple cider vinegar
- 3 ounces tomato paste
- 1 teaspoon hot sauce
- 1/8 teaspoon horseradish
- Pinch of mustard powder
- Pinch of salt & pepper
- Stevia
- Water
- Cocktail dipping sauce

Directions:

Combine spices, tomato paste, horseradish, lemon juice and vinegar together and marinate, dipping sauce to chill. Add more water to desired consistency. Steam shrimp until pink.

Cool shrimp for about 30 minutes in the refrigerator. Serve with cocktail dipping sauce.

Nutritional Information per Serving:

Calories: 193; Total Fat: 2.1 g; Carbs: 17.9 g; Dietary Fiber: 3.5 g; Sugars: 10.5 g; Protein: 26.5 g; Cholesterol: 211 mg; Sodium: 457 mg

Chilled Garlicky Pickles

Yield: 1 Serving
Total Time: 10 Minutes
Prep Time: 10 Minutes
Cook Time: N/A

Ingredients

- ½ cup apple cider vinegar
- 1 cucumber, sliced
- 4 cloves garlic, sliced
- 3 tablespoons fresh lemon juice
- Pinch of salt

Directions:

Combine all liquid ingredients. Add salt to cucumber slices. Stack sliced cucumber tightly in a small glass jar putting garlic slices in between cucumber layers. Pour lemon juice and apple cider vinegar into the glass jar until all the cucumber slices ate covered. Cool within a refrigerator overnight for nearly four days.

Nutritional Information per Serving:

Calories: 99; Total Fat: 0.8 g; Carbs: 17 g; Dietary Fiber: 1.9 g; Sugars: 6.6 g; Protein: 3.1 g; Cholesterol: 0 mg; Sodium: 178 mg

Tasty Apple Slaw

Yield: 1-2 Servings
Total Time: 10 Minutes
Prep Time: 10 Minutes
Cook Time: N/A

Ingredients

- ½ head cabbage
- 1 apple diced
- 1 tablespoon apple cider vinegar
- 2 tablespoons fresh lemon juice
- Pinch of mustard powder
- Pinch of cinnamon
- ¼ teaspoon garlic powder
- Stevia
- Pinch of salt & pepper

Directions:

Shred the cabbage and mix with spices and lemon juice. Marinate for at least 30 minutes. Add apples and cinnamon.

Phase 3 modifications: Stir in Greek yogurt or mayonnaise.

Nutritional Information per Serving:

Calories: 156; Total Fat: 1.9 g; Carbs: 32.2 g; Dietary Fiber: 12.1; Sugars: 17.8 g; Protein: 2.7 g; Cholesterol: 0 mg; Sodium: 245 mg

Cerviche

Yield: 1 Serving
Total Time: 20 Minutes
Prep Time: 10 Minutes
Cook Time: 10 Minutes

Ingredients

- 100 grams cooked shrimp
- 1 minced clove of garlic
- Diced tomatoes
- 3 tablespoons fresh lemon juice
- Hot sauce
- Salt and pepper
- Fresh chopped cilantro

Directions:

Steam the fish or shrimp. Add chopped cilantro, lemon, garlic and onion.

Add hot sauce and diced tomatoes and stir. Chill and refrigerate the ingredients.

Phase 3 modifications: Add other seafood and diced jalapeno and serve over cream cheese.

Nutritional Information per Serving:

Calories: 152; Total Fat: 2.3 g; Carbs: 7.3 g; Dietary Fiber: 1.7; Sugars: 4.2 g; Protein: 24.2 g; Cholesterol: 211 mg; Sodium: 259 mg

Melba Toast w/ Strawberry Jam

Yield: 1 Serving
Total Time: 10 Minutes
Prep Time: 10 Minutes
Cook Time: N/A

Ingredients

- Stevia
- 1 Melba toast
- 8 strawberries

Directions:

Puree the strawberries with stevia. To obtain a crunchy texture, add crushed Melba toast on top of the strawberry puree or serve Melba toast topped with the puree.

Variations: Add cinnamon of vanilla powder to toast for more flavor.

Nutritional Information per Serving:

Calories: 55; Total Fat: 0.6 g; Carbs: 11 g; Dietary Fiber: 2.1 g; Sugars: 5.1 g; Protein: 1.3 g; Cholesterol: 0 mg; Sodium: 62 mg

Melba Toast Croutons

Yield: 1 Serving
Total Time: 15 Minutes
Prep Time: 10 Minutes
Cook Time: 5 Minutes

Ingredients

- Pinch of paprika
- 2 tablespoons fresh lemon juice
- Pinch of ground nutmeg
- Pinch of onion powder
- Pinch of garlic powder
- Pinch of cinnamon
- Stevia
- 1 serving Melba toast
- Pinch of salt & pepper

Directions:

Sprinkle Melba toast with spices and lemon juice and dust dry with spices or bake in an oven for about 5 minutes over 350 degree heat.

Nutritional Information per Serving:

Calories: 72; Total Fat: 0.8 g; Carbs: 21.7 g; Dietary Fiber: 8.2 g; Sugars: 12.1 g; Protein: 3.1 g; Cholesterol: 21 mg; Sodium: 216 mg

Toast with Spicy Cucumber

Yield: 1 Serving
Total Time: 10 Minutes
Prep Time: 10 Minutes
Cook Time: N/A

Ingredients

- 2 to 3 slices of cucumber
- Pinch of cayenne or chili pepper
- 1 red onion, minced
- 1 tablespoon apple cider vinegar
- 1 Melba toast
- 1 teaspoon onion powder
- 1 teaspoon garlic powder
- Pinch of salt & pepper

Directions:

Mix the apple cider vinegar with spices. Allow cucumber slices to marinate in the spice mixture. Sprinkle Melba toast with onion after topping with cucumber.

Variations: Sprinkle with crumbs and serve.

Nutritional Information per Serving:

Calories: 96; Total Fat: 1.2 g; Carbs: 23.4 g; Dietary Fiber: 8.9 g; Sugars: 14.2 g; Protein: 2.1 g; Cholesterol: 0 mg; Sodium: 230 mg

HCG Dressings, Sauces, Marinades & Spice Blends

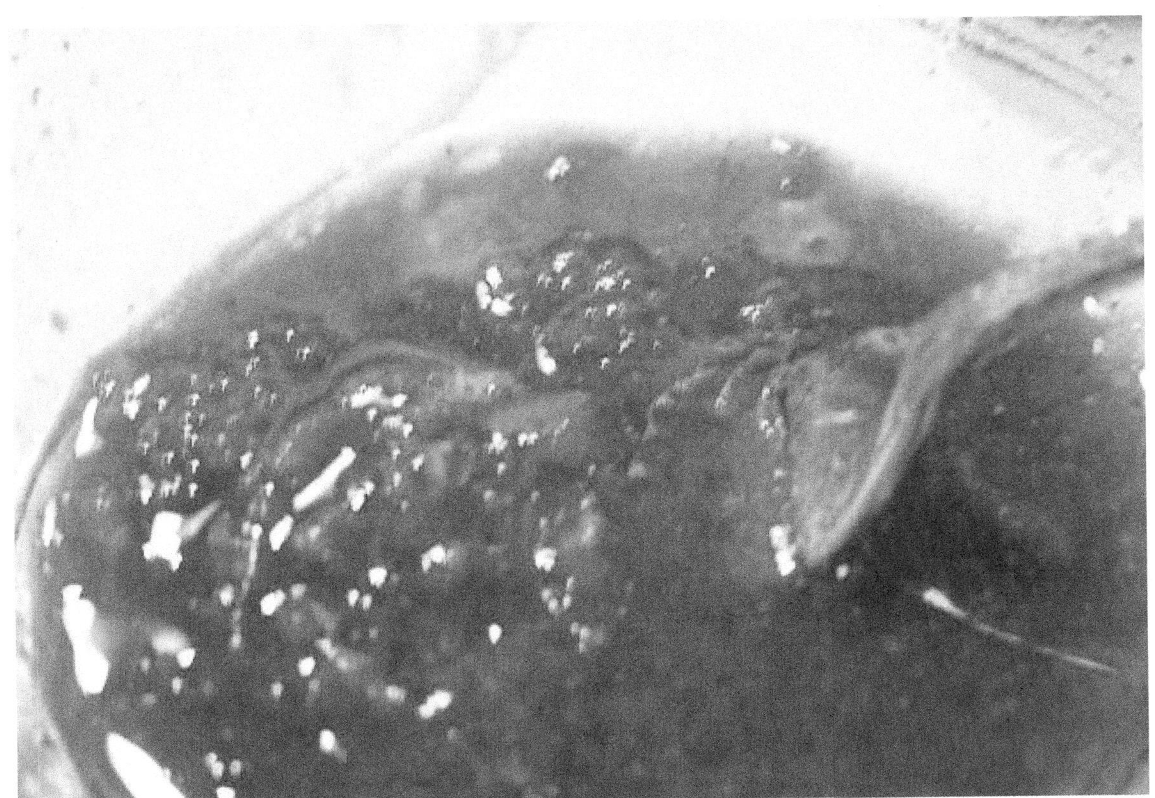

Yield: 1 Serving
Total Time: 10 Minutes
Prep Time: 10 Minutes
Cook Time: N/A

Strawberry Vinaigrette

Ingredients

- 8 strawberries
- 1 teaspoon fresh lemon juice
- 1 teaspoon apple cider vinegar
- Pinch of salt & pepper
- Pinch of cayenne
- Stevia

Directions:

In a food processor, mix all ingredients until smooth. Add green salad or fresh arugula. Garnish with black pepper and strawberries slices.

Variations: use as a marinade or sauce for chicken.

Nutritional Information per Serving:

Calories: 58; Total Fat: 2.1 g; Carbs: 37.4 g; Dietary Fiber: 6.3 g; Sugars: 25.6 g; Protein: 4.3 g; Cholesterol: 0 mg; Sodium: 0 mg

Tarragon-Orange Marinade for Fish & Chicken

Yield: 1 Serving
Total Time: 10 Minutes
Prep Time: 10 Minutes
Cook Time: N/A

Ingredients

- 1 teaspoon chopped fresh tarragon
- 1 clove of garlic, minced
- 2 tablespoons apple cider vinegar
- ¼ cup vegetable or chicken broth
- 2 tablespoons fresh orange juice
- ¼ teaspoon onion powder
- Pinch of salt & pepper

Directions:

Mix the spices with liquid ingredients and cook for about 3 minutes and then cool. Allow fish or chicken to marinate for at least 20 minutes before cooking. Add a little water periodically. Put the sauce aside and add apple cider vinegar to make more dressing for a salad. Serve with vegetable or mixed green salad.

Nutritional Information per Serving:

Calories: 111; Total Fat: 2.1 g; Carbs: 37.4 g; Dietary Fiber: 6.3 g; Sugars: 28.1 g; Protein: 4.3 g; Cholesterol: 0 mg; Sodium: 231 mg

Tarragon Vinegar Infusion

Yield: 4 Servings
Total Time: 10 Minutes
Prep Time: 10 Minutes
Cook Time: N/A

Ingredients

- 1 cup tarragon
- ¼ cup apple cider vinegar
- Pinch of salt & pepper

Directions:

In a jar, combine the fresh tarragon with vinegar. Shake vigorously and set aside overnight for the flavors to infuse into the apple cider vinegar. Use as a dressing or marinade for fish.

Nutritional Information per Serving:

Calories: 98; Total Fat: 2.1 g; Carbs: 15 g; Dietary Fiber: 2.1 g; Sugars: 0.2 g; Protein: 6.6 g; Cholesterol: 0 mg; Sodium: 211 mg

Citrus Ginger Dressing

Yield: 1-2 Serving
Total Time: 10 Minutes
Prep Time: 10 Minutes
Cook Time: N/A

Ingredients

- Fresh ginger
- 2 tablespoons fresh orange juice
- 1 tablespoon Bragg's liquid aminos
- 1 tablespoon fresh lemon juice
- 1 tsp apple cider vinegar
- Pinch of salt & pepper
- Stevia

Directions:

Mix all liquid ingredients with spices. Use as marinade with double the recipe or serve over salad. Warm lightly to infuse flavors.

Nutritional Information per Serving:

Calories: 38; Total Fat: 0.5 g; Carbs: 7.5 g; Dietary Fiber: 0.8 g; Sugars: 3.1 g; Protein: 0.8 g; Cholesterol: 0 mg; Sodium: 5 mg

Teriyaki Sauce

Yield: 1-2 Servings
Total Time: 30 Minutes
Prep Time: 10 Minutes
Cook Time: 20 Minutes

Ingredients

- 2 teaspoon apple cider vinegar
- 1 tablespoon minced onion
- ¼ cup fresh lemon juice
- ¼ cup Bragg's liquid aminos
- 1 clove minced garlic
- 1 teaspoon onion powder
- 1 teaspoon garlic powder
- 1 cup fresh orange juice
- ½ cup chicken or beef broth
- ½ teaspoon grated or powdered ginger
- 1 teaspoon orange or lemon zest
- Stevia

Directions:

In a small pan combine all ingredients and heat until boiled. Simmer over low heat for about 20 minutes. The longer you simmer the richer the flavors. Add broth or water if the liquid is reduced in order to infuse the flavors. Serve as sauce with beef or chicken or as glaze.

Nutritional Information per Serving:

Calories: 22; Total Fat: 1.9 g; Carbs: 2.2 g; Dietary Fiber: 0.8 g; Sugars: 1.1 g; Protein: 0.7 g; Cholesterol: 0 mg; Sodium: 19 mg

Horseradish Marinade

Yield: 1-2 Servings
Total Time: 10 Minutes
Prep Time: 10 Minutes
Cook Time: N/A

Ingredients

- ½ teaspoon garlic powder
- ¼ cup beef broth
- ¼ teaspoon paprika
- 1 teaspoon of horseradish

Directions:

Whip the ingredients and heat in a saucepan. Use as a marinade or sauce and serve with beef.

Nutritional Information per Serving:

Calories: 18; Total Fat: 0.5 g; Carbs: 2.1 g; Dietary Fiber: 0.5 g; Sugars: 1 g; Protein: 1.6 g; Cholesterol: 0 mg; Sodium: 207 mg

Yield: 2 Servings

Total Time: 70 Minutes

Prep Time: 10 Minutes

Cook Time: 60 Minutes

Marinara Sauce

Ingredients

- 1 teaspoon dried oregano
- 1 tablespoon fresh chopped or dried basil
- Cayenne pepper
- 1 cup vegetable or chicken broth
- 2 red onions, minced
- Pinch of salt & pepper
- 1 6 ounce tomato paste
- Marjoram
- 4 large tomatoes
- 2 cloves garlic, minced

Directions:

In a food processor, chop and grind the tomatoes into puree. Heat in a saucepan, adding spices. Simmer for 30- 60minutes. You may add water to a desired consistency.

Nutritional Information per Serving:

Calories: 23; Total Fat: 0.8 g; Carbs: 5.4 g; Dietary Fiber: 2.7 g; Sugars: 2.3 g; Protein: 1.1 g; Cholesterol: 0 mg; Sodium: 217 mg

Tomato Picante Dressing

Yield: 2-4 Servings
Total Time: 10 Minutes
Prep Time: 10 Minutes
Cook Time: N/A

Ingredients

- 2 tablespoon fresh lemon juice
- ½ teaspoon chili powder
- 1 teaspoon mustard powder
- Pinch of salt & black pepper
- 1 chopped tomato
- 1 tablespoon apple cider vinegar
- ½ teaspoon ground cumin
- 1 clove garlic chopped
- 1 cup tomato sauce
- Cayenne pepper

Directions:

In a food processor, puree the garlic and tomato. Add cumin, cayenne, mustard, chili powder, tomato sauce, lemon juice and salt. Blend to make it smooth and refrigerate. Stir before use.

Nutritional Information per Serving:

Calories: 38; Total Fat: 0.8 g; Carbs: 5.2 g; Dietary Fiber: 1.7 g; Sugars: 4.1 g; Protein: 1.2 g; Cholesterol: 0 mg; Sodium: 216 mg

Grapefruit Vinaigrette

Yield: 1-2 Servings
Total Time: 10 Minutes
Prep Time: 10 Minutes
Cook Time: N/A

Ingredients

- 1 tablespoon fresh lemon juice
- 2 tablespoons grapefruit juice
- 1 teaspoon apple cider vinegar
- Stevia

Directions:

Mix vinegar with the juices and add stevia. Pour onto mixed green salad and top with grapefruit parts. Use as marinade chicken, fish or shrimp. Add salt and pepper.

Nutritional Information per Serving:

Calories: 14; Total Fat: 0.2 g; Carbs: 2.7 g; Dietary Fiber: 0.4 g; Sugars: 2.4 g; Protein: 0.3 g; Cholesterol: 0 mg; Sodium: 3 mg

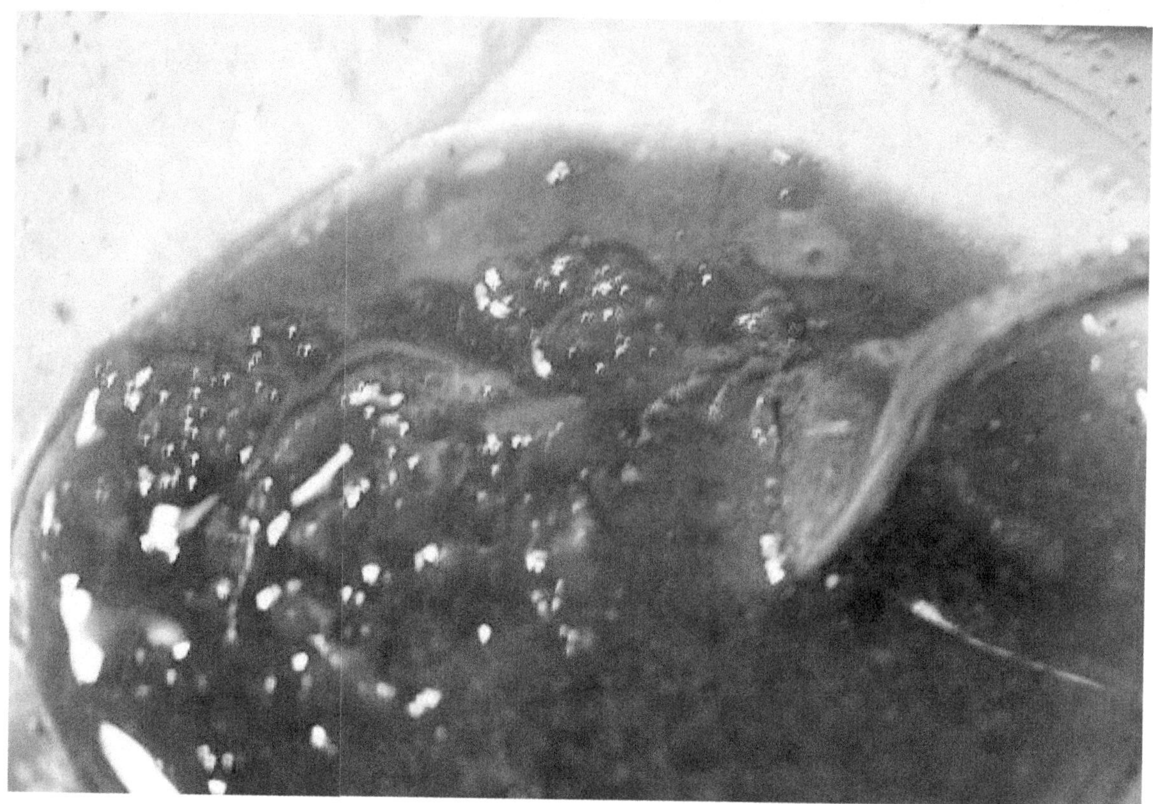

Tomato Basil Vinaigrette

Yield: 2-3 Servings
Total Time: 20 Minutes
Prep Time: 10 Minutes
Cook Time: 10 Minutes

Ingredients

- ¼ cup vegetable broth
- 1 tablespoon minced onion
- 3 tablespoons tomato paste
- 1/8 teaspoon oregano
- 2 tablespoons fresh lemon juice
- 3 tablespoons apple cider vinegar
- ½ teaspoon onion powder
- 1 tsp dried basil
- ½ teaspoon garlic powder
- Cayenne pepper
- Stevia

Directions:

In a saucepan, combine all ingredients and heat lightly until boiled. Add a little broth or water as desired. Chill and serve over salad with black pepper.

Nutritional Information per Serving:

Calories: 17; Total Fat: 0.1 g; Carbs: 3.2 g; Dietary Fiber: 1.7 g; Sugars: 1 g; Protein: 0.8 g; Cholesterol: 0 mg; Sodium: 216 mg

Italian Vinaigrette

Yield: 2 Servings
Total Time: 15 Minutes
Prep Time: 10 Minutes
Cook Time: 5 Minutes

Ingredients

- 2 tablespoons fresh lemon juice
- 2 red onion, minced
- ½ teaspoon onion powder
- 2 tablespoons apple cider vinegar
- ½ teaspoon garlic powder
- 1 teaspoon Italian herb spice
- ½ cup vegetable broth

Directions:

In a saucepan, mix all ingredients. Heat over low heat for 5 minutes to infuse flavors. Remove from heat and cool. Use as marinade and serve as dressing.

Phase 3 modifications: Replace lemon juice with mayonnaise or sour cream or add olive oil.

Nutritional Information per Serving:

Calories: 33; Total Fat: 1.2 g; Carbs: 3.1 g; Dietary Fiber: 0.8 g; Sugars: 1.3 g; Protein: 0.8 g; Cholesterol: 0 mg; Sodium: 222 mg

Hot Cajun Dipping Sauce

Yield: 1-2 Servings
Total Time: 10 Minutes
Prep Time: 10 Minutes
Cook Time: N/A

Ingredients

- 1 teaspoon onion powder
- 1 tablespoon lemon juice
- ¼ teaspoon Old Bay seasoning mix
- Stevia
- Pinch of cayenne pepper
- 1 teaspoon garlic powder
- Pinch of salt and black pepper
- 3 tablespoons apple cider vinegar

Directions:

In a small bowl, mix ingredients and pour on to salad. You can use as a marinade for fish or vegetables or serve as sauce.

Nutritional Information per Serving:

Calories: 19; Total Fat: 0.4 g; Carbs: 2.1 g; Dietary Fiber: 0.6 g; Sugars: 1.2 g; Protein: 1.2 g; Cholesterol: 0 mg; Sodium: 216 mg

Healthy Salsa

Yield: 1-2 Serving
Total Time: 10 Minutes
Prep Time: 10 Minutes
Cook Time: N/A

Ingredients

- 3 tablespoons lemon juice
- 1 tablespoon apple cider vinegar
- 2 tablespoons chopped onion
- 2 cloves garlic, minced
- ¼ teaspoon dried or fresh
- Pinch of cayenne pepper
- Fresh chopped cilantro
- 1 cup chopped tomato
- Salt and pepper
- ¼ teaspoon chili powder

Directions:

In a food processor, puree the ingredients to obtain smooth salsa. Add spices and refrigerate for at least 10 minutes.

Phase 3 modifications: Add chipotle or jalapeno peppers and mix in avocado to make tasty guacamole.

Nutritional Information per Serving:

Calories: 22; Total Fat: 0.3 g; Carbs: 3.3 g; Dietary Fiber: 1.1 g; Sugars: 1.1 g; Protein: 0.8 g; Cholesterol: 0 mg; Sodium: 231 mg

Barbeque Sauce

Yield: 1-2 Servings
Total Time: 15 Minutes
Prep Time: 10 Minutes
Cook Time: 5 Minutes

Ingredients

- 3 tablespoons fresh lemon juice
- ½ teaspoon garlic powder
- ½ teaspoon Worcestershire sauce
- 1 teaspoon chopped parsley
- ¼ teaspoon chili powder
- 1 tablespoon hot sauce
- Cayenne pepper
- Liquid smoke hickory flavoring
- Water
- 1 tablespoon minced onion
- 3 ounces tomato paste
- Stevia
- ½ teaspoon onion powder
- 3 cloves minced garlic
- ¼ cup apple cider vinegar
- Salt & pepper

Directions:

Mix all the ingredients in a saucepan and heat until boiled. Add a little water and simmer for 5 minutes or more. Use as a grilling sauce for beef or chicken.

Nutritional Information per Serving:

Calories: 97; Total Fat: 2.2 g; Carbs: 12.1 g; Dietary Fiber: 2.7 g; Sugars: 9.1 g; Protein: 1.8 g; Cholesterol: 0 mg; Sodium: 218 mg

Marinated Apple Relish

Yield: 1 Serving
Total Time: 10 Minutes
Prep Time: 10 Minutes
Cook Time: N/A

Ingredients

- 1 apple, pureed
- 2 tablespoons apple cider vinegar
- Worcestershire sauce
- 1 stalk minced celery
- ½ red onion, minced
- Pinch of salt & pepper
- 2 tablespoons fresh lemon juice
- Stevia

Directions:

Combine celery and apples together. Mix the spice with liquid ingredients until dissolved and add to the apple mixture. Mix thoroughly and marinate the ingredients for at least 30 minutes until the flavors blend.

Nutritional Information per Serving:

Calories: 177; Total Fat: 1.7 g; Carbs: 31.4 g; Dietary Fiber: 7.7 g; Sugars: 23.4 g; Protein: 2.3 g; Cholesterol: 0 mg; Sodium: 218 mg

Sweet Wasabi Marinade

Yield: 1 Serving
Total Time: 10 Minutes
Prep Time: 10 Minutes
Cook Time: N/A

Ingredients

- 1 tablespoon fresh lemon juice
- Stevia
- 2 tablespoons Bragg's liquid aminos
- ¼ teaspoon wasabi powder

Directions:

Combine wasabi with Bragg's and add stevia and lemon juice.

Nutritional Information per Serving:

Calories: 15; Total Fat: 0.3 g; Carbs: 2.1 g; Dietary Fiber: 0.6 g; Sugars: 1.2 g; Protein: 0.7 g; Cholesterol: 0 mg; Sodium: 14 mg

Sweet & Spicy Mustard Dressing

Yield: 1-2 Servings
Total Time: 15 Minutes
Prep Time: 10 Minutes
Cook Time: 5 Minutes

Ingredients

- 2 tablespoons fresh lemon juice
- 1 clove garlic, minced
- 1 tablespoon minced onion
- 1 tablespoon Bragg's liquid aminos
- 2 tablespoons homemade mustard
- 2 tablespoons apple cider vinegar
- Pinch of turmeric
- Stevia
- Water

Directions:

Mix spices with liquid ingredients thoroughly and heat over low heat in a saucepan. Add more vinegar or water to obtain a desired consistency.

Nutritional Information per Serving:

Calories: 23; Total Fat: 0.3 g; Carbs: 3 g; Dietary Fiber: 0.5 g; Sugars: 1.2 g; Protein: 0.6 g; Cholesterol: 0 mg; Sodium: 9 mg

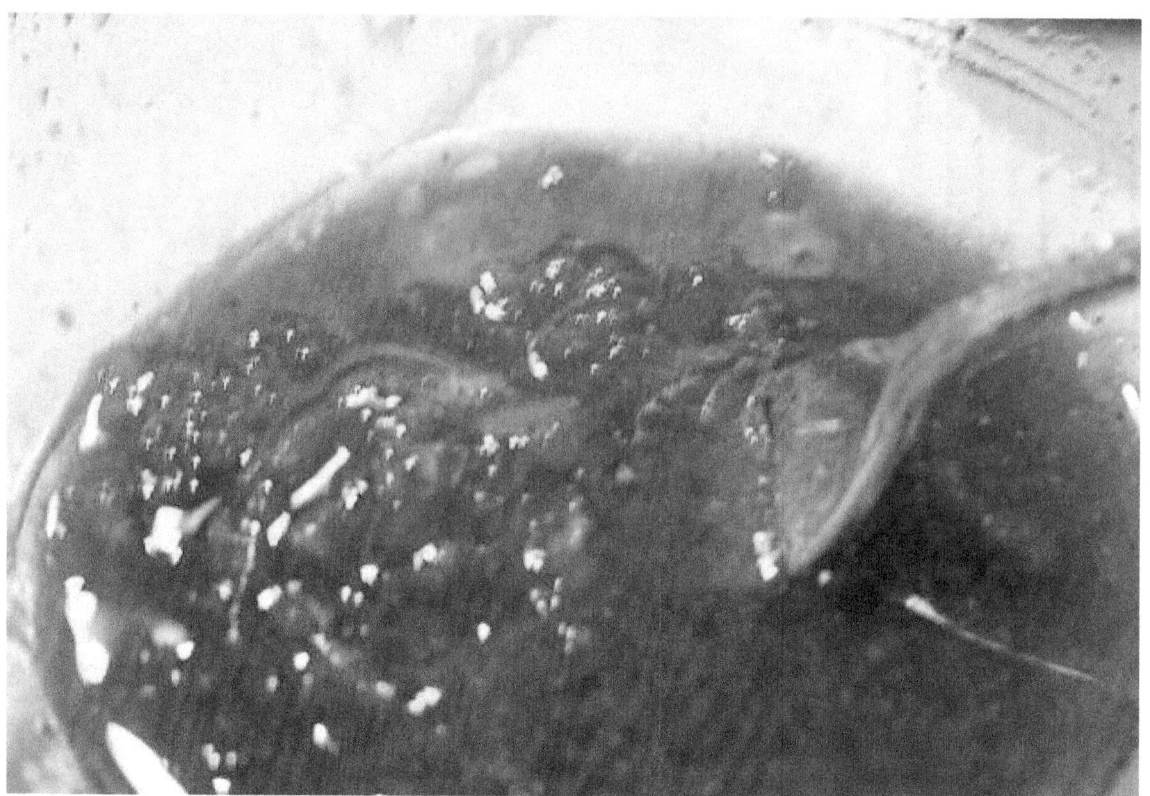

Lemon Pepper Marinade

Yield: 1-2 Servings
Total Time: 10 Minutes
Prep Time: 10 Minutes
Cook Time: N/A

Ingredients

- 3 tablespoons vegetable broth
- 4 tablespoons fresh lemon juice
- Stevia
- Pinch of salt and pepper

Directions:

Combine all the ingredients together. Allow them to marinate for at least 20 minutes.

Nutritional Information per Serving:

Calories: 11; Total Fat: 0.1 g; Carbs: 2.3 g; Dietary Fiber: 0.7 g; Sugars: 1.1 g; Protein: 0.8 g; Cholesterol: 0 mg; Sodium: 216 mg

Spicy Orange Sauce

Yield: 1-2 Servings
Total Time: 25 Minutes
Prep Time: 15 Minutes
Cook Time: 10 Minutes

Ingredients

- 2 tablespoons fresh orange juice
- 2 tablespoons fresh lemon juice
- 1 clove garlic, minced
- 1 tablespoon minced green onion
- ¼ teaspoon ginger powder
- 1 teaspoon lemon & orange zest
- ¼ teaspoon garlic powder
- ½ cup water
- Stevia
- Pinch of cayenne pepper

Directions:

Add water, the slightly juiced lemon and orange, both with rind, in a saucepan. Allow the ingredients to boil. Simmer over lower heat and add water to obtain required consistency. Heat lightly until the pulp is separated from the rinds. Throw away the rinds. Stir continuously, then add stevia, spices and onion. Add beef, chicken or white fish and pour the orange sauce or sauté to brown. Garnish with rest of orange slices.

Nutritional Information per Serving:

Calories: 41; Total Fat: 0.7 g; Carbs: 7.2 g; Dietary Fiber: 2.1 g; Sugars: 4.4 g; Protein: 1.3 g; Cholesterol: 0 mg; Sodium: 216 mg

Chinese 5 Spice (Version One)

Yield: 4 Servings
Total Time: 10 Minutes
Prep Time: 10 Minutes
Cook Time: N/A

Ingredients

- 3 tablespoons cinnamon
- 2 teaspoons ground anise seed
- 2 teaspoons ground fennel seed
- 1 ½ teaspoons Szechuan
- 1 ½ teaspoons crushed Peppercorns or black peppercorns
- ¾ teaspoon ground cloves

Directions:

Mix together all the spices until well combined. Use the spice blend on meat, fish, chicken, etc.

Nutritional Information per Serving:

Calories: 25; Total Fat: 0.5 g; Carbs: 6.4 g; Dietary Fiber: 3.8 g; Sugars: 0.1 g; Protein: 0.7 g; Cholesterol: 0 mg; Sodium: 3 mg

Yield: 1 Serving
Total Time: 10 Minutes
Prep Time: 10 Minutes
Cook Time: N/A

Chinese 5 Spice Blend (Version Two)

Ingredients

- 1 teaspoon ground Star Anise
- 1 ¼ teaspoon ground fennel seeds
- ½ teaspoon cinnamon
- 1 teaspoon Szechuan or ground peppercorns
- ½ teaspoon ground cloves
- ½ teaspoon sea salt
- ¼ teaspoon white pepper

Directions:

Mix together all the spices. Use as desired.

Nutritional Information per Serving:

Calories: 29; Total Fat: 8 g; Carbs: 5.6 g; Dietary Fiber: 3 g; Sugars: 0.1 g; Protein: 1.2 g; Cholesterol: 0 mg; Sodium: 942 mg

Chinese 5 Spice Blend (Version Three)

Yield: 4 Servings
Total Time: 10 Minutes
Prep Time: 10 Minutes
Cook Time: N/A

Ingredients

- 2 tablespoons ground Star Anise
- 2 tablespoons ground fennel seeds
- 2 teaspoon crushed cassia or cinnamon
- 2 teaspoons ground or Szechuan or crushed peppercorns
- ¼ teaspoon ground cloves

Directions:

Mix together all the spices. Use as desired.

Nutritional Information per Serving:

Calories: 27; Total Fat: 1 g; Carbs: 4.9 g; Dietary Fiber: 2.6 g; Sugars: 0 g; Protein: 1.2 g; Cholesterol: 0 mg; Sodium: 4 mg

Scrumptious Chicken Gravy

Yield: 1 Serving

Total Time: 25 Minutes

Prep Time: 10 Minutes

Cook Time: 15 Minutes

Ingredients

- 1 grissini breadstick
- ½ cup vegetable broth
- poultry seasoning to taste

Directions:

In a food processor, grind breadstick into a fine powder.

In a small saucepan, bring ¼ cup of vegetable broth to a gentle boil; stir in grissini powder until dissolved. While stirring, gradually add in the remaining broth and lower heat to a simmer. Simmer for about 3-5 minutes or until the gravy is thick.

Stir in poultry seasoning and serve right away!

Nutritional Information per Serving:

Calories: 60; Total Fat: 1.7 g; Carbs: 6.6 g; Dietary Fiber: 0 g; Sugars: 0.4 g; Protein: 3.4 g; Cholesterol: 0 mg; Sodium: 422 mg

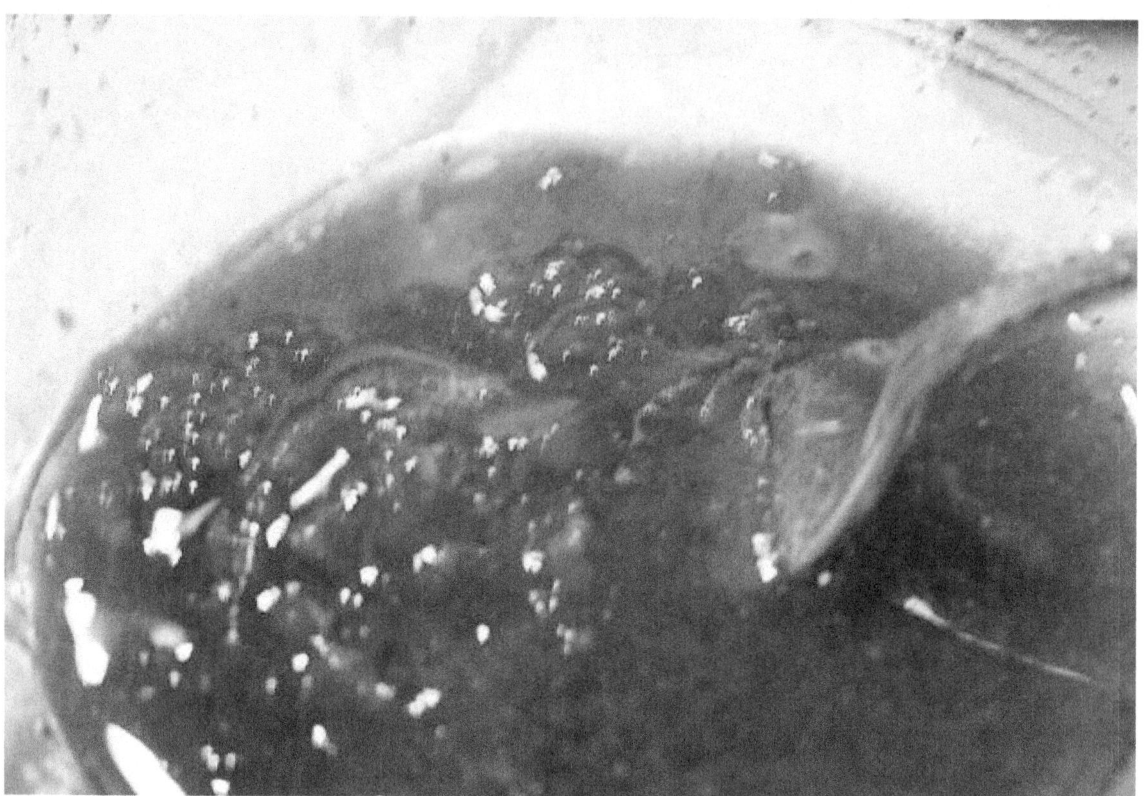

Sweet & Sour Salad Dressing

Yield: 2 Servings
Total Time: 10 Minutes
Prep Time: 10 Minutes
Cook Time: N/A

Ingredients

- 3 tablespoons apple cider vinegar
- ½ packet stevia
- 1/4 teaspoon sea salt
- 1/4 teaspoon pepper

Directions:

In a small bowl, whisk together all the ingredients until well blended.

Drizzle the dressing over salad greens, stir fry or spinach.

Nutritional Information per Serving:

Calories: 5; Total Fat: 0 g; Carbs: 0.4 g; Dietary Fiber: 0.1 g; Sugars: 0.1 g; Protein: 0 g; Cholesterol: 0 mg; Sodium: 235 mg

Taco seasoning

Yield: 2 Servings
Total Time: 10 Minutes
Prep Time: 10 Minutes
Cook Time: N/A

Ingredients

- 1 teaspoon oregano
- 1 teaspoon paprika
- 1 teaspoon garlic powder
- 1 teaspoon cumin
- 2 teaspoons onion powder
- 1 tablespoon chili powder

Directions:

Mix together all ingredients and use as desired. Store the rest in an airtight container.

Nutritional Information per Serving:

Calories: 34; Total Fat: 1.1 g; Carbs: 6.5 g; Dietary Fiber: 4.4 g; Sugars: 1.67 g; Protein: 1.4 g; Cholesterol: 0 mg; Sodium: 42 mg

Chicken Broth Base

Yield: 8 Servings
Total Time: 45 Minutes
Prep Time: 10 Minutes
Cook Time: 35 Minutes

Ingredients

- 24 ounces boneless skinless chicken breast
- 9 cups water
- 1 teaspoon garlic powder
- ½ teaspoon onion powder
- ½ teaspoon celery powder
- 1 teaspoon poultry seasoning
- 1 teaspoon pepper
- 1 tablespoon sea salt

Directions:

In a large pot, combine all the ingredients and bring to a gentle boil. Lower heat and simmer for about 30 minutes or until chicken is cooked through; remove chicken to use for other meals and free the broth in small containers to use later.

Nutritional Information per Serving:

Calories: 165; Total Fat: 6.3 g; Carbs: 0.7 g; Dietary Fiber: 0.1 g; Sugars: 0.2; Protein: 24.7 g; Cholesterol: 76 mg; Sodium: 748 mg

Multi Marinade Dressing

Yield: 8 Servings
Total Time: 10 Minutes
Prep Time: 10 Minutes
Cook Time: N/A

Ingredients

- 2/3 cup apple cider vinegar
- 1/3 cup fresh lemon juice
- 1 tablespoon water
- 1/2 teaspoon garlic powder
- 1/4 teaspoon sea salt
- 1 teaspoon dried shallots
- 1/2 teaspoon onion powder
- 1 teaspoon cilantro
- 1 teaspoon parsley
- 1 teaspoon basil
- orange or plain stevia

Directions:

Mix together all the ingredients and use as marinade or dressing.

Nutritional Information per Serving:

Calories: 19; Total Fat: 0.1 g; Carbs: 3.4 g; Dietary Fiber: 0.6 g; Sugars: 2.5 g; Protein: 0.4 g; Cholesterol: 0 mg; Sodium: 62 mg

Veggie Marinade

Yield: 1 Serving
Total Time: 10 Minutes
Prep Time: 10 Minutes
Cook Time: N/A

Ingredients

- ½ juice of Lemon
- Garlic
- Sea Salt
- Pepper

Directions:

Whisk together all the ingredients; use as marinade for steamed veggies.

Nutritional Information per Serving:

Calories: 11; Total Fat: 0.1 g; Carbs: 3.2 g; Dietary Fiber: 0.2 g; Sugars: 2.9 g; Protein: 0.3 g; Cholesterol: 0 mg; Sodium: 267 mg

Yield: 1 Serving

Total Time: 10 Minutes

Prep Time: 10 Minutes

Cook Time: N/A

Steak marinade

Ingredients

- 1 teaspoon fresh lemon juice
- finely chopped fresh cilantro
- 1 teaspoon Chinese Spice Blend
- 1-1/2 teaspoon chili powder

Directions:

Mix together all the ingredients; rub into steak and marinate for at least 1 hour before cooking.

Nutritional Information per Serving:

Calories: 19; Total Fat: 0.5 g; Carbs: 1.7 g; Dietary Fiber: 0.9 g; Sugars: 0.3 g; Protein: 44.4 g; Cholesterol: 0 mg; Sodium: 27 mg

HCG Diet Beverages

Yield: 1 Serving

Total Time: 15 Minutes

Prep Time: 5 Minutes

Cook Time: 10 Minutes

Iced Tea

Ingredients

- 6 ounces hot water
- ½ cup cranberry juice
- 1 bag Chamomile tea
- 1 gram Yerba mate
- 1 tablespoon peppermint
- 1 tablespoon vanilla Chai spice
- Stevia

Directions:

Brew tea and refrigerate; stir in stevia and serve over ice garnsihed with mint.

Nutritional Information per Serving:

Calories: 60; Total Fat: 1.6 g; Carbs: 9.5 g; Dietary Fiber: 1.8 g; Sugars: 6 g; Protein: 0.4 g; Cholesterol: 0 mg; Sodium: 38 mg

Sparkling Virgin Apple Martini/Caramel Apple Martini

Yield: 1 Serving
Total Time: 5 Minutes
Prep Time: 5 Minutes
Cook Time: N/A

Ingredients

- 1 apple, juiced
- 2 tablespoons fresh lemon juice
- 6 ounces sparkling mineral water, chilled
- Vanilla liquid stevia
- Crushed ice
- Apple slice

Directions:

Mix all ingredients and serve over ice garnished with apple slice.

Phase 3 modifications: Add a shot of vodka

Nutritional Information per Serving:

Calories: 79; Total Fat: 1.8 g; Carbs: 10.1 g; Dietary Fiber: 2.4 g; Sugars: 6.7 g; Protein: 1.4 g; Cholesterol: 0 mg; Sodium: 42 mg

Refreshing Grapefruit Virgin Martini

Yield: 1 Serving
Total Time: 5 Minutes
Prep Time: 5 Minutes
Cook Time: N/A

Ingredients

- 2 tablespoons fresh grapefruit juice
- 5 ounces sparkling mineral water
- Vanilla stevia
- Ice

Directions:

Stir together all ingredients and serve over ice.

Phase 3 modifications: Add a shot of vodka

Nutritional Information per Serving:

Calories: 21Total Fat: 0.2 g; Carbs: 1.9 g; Dietary Fiber: 0.4 g; Sugars: 0.7 g; Protein: 0.2 g; Cholesterol: 0 mg; Sodium: 27 mg

Bloody Hot Thin Mary

Yield: 1 Serving
Total Time: 5 Minutes
Prep Time: 5 Minutes
Cook Time: N/A

Ingredients

- 8 ounces fresh tomato juice
- 2 tablespoons fresh lemon juice
- 2 tablespoons apple cider vinegar
- Pinch of cayenne pepper
- 3 dashes Worcestershire sauce
- 1 teaspoon hot sauce
- Freshly ground black pepper
- Celery salt

Directions:

Stir together all ingredients and serve over ice.

Variations: Stir in ¼ teaspoon of horseradish.

Phase 3 modifications: Add a shot of vodka

Nutritional Information per Serving:

Calories: 67; Total Fat: 1.7 g; Carbs: 8.1 g; Dietary Fiber: 1.4 g; Sugars: 3.7 g; Protein: 1.5 g; Cholesterol: 0 mg; Sodium: 61 mg

Hot Apple Cider

Yield: 1 Serving
Total Time: 15 Minutes
Prep Time: 5 Minutes
Cook Time: 10 Minutes

Ingredients

- 1 apple, juiced
- 2 tablespoons fresh lemon juice
- 1 tablespoon apple cider vinegar
- Water
- Pinch of lemon zest
- Pinch of clove
- Pinch of allspice
- Pinch of nutmeg
- ¼ teaspoon cinnamon
- Stevia

Directions:

Combine all ingredients and heat in a saucepan; serve hot garnished with cinnamon stick.

Nutritional Information per Serving:

Calories: 131; Total Fat: 0.8 g; Carbs: 32.6 g; Dietary Fiber: 6.1 g; Sugars: 24 g; Protein: 0.9 g; Cholesterol: 0 mg; Sodium: 10 mg

Lemon or Strawberry Ice Cubes

Yield: 1 Serving
Total Time: 5 Minutes
Prep Time: 5 Minutes
Cook Time: N/A

Ingredients

- 6 strawberries
- Chopped mint
- ¼ cup water
- Stevia

Directions:

Puree all ingredients and free in molds until firm. Add to teas, cold drinks or recipes for an extra flavor.

Nutritional Information per Serving:

Calories: 23; Total Fat: 0.2 g; Carbs: 5.5 g; Dietary Fiber: 1.4 g; Sugars: 3.5 g; Protein: 0.5 g; Cholesterol: 0 mg; Sodium: 3 mg

Mint Chocolate Coffee Smoothie

Yield: 1 Serving
Total Time: 5 Minutes
Prep Time: 5 Minutes
Cook Time: N/A

Ingredients

- 6 ounces brewed coffee, chilled
- 1 tablespoon milk
- ¼ teaspoon cocoa powder
- Dark chocolate stevia
- Peppermint stevia
- Ice cubes

Directions:

Blend all ingredients until very smooth. Serve garnished with mint.

Phase 3 modifications: Add cream or half and half.

Nutritional Information per Serving:

Calories: 39; Total Fat: 4.8 g; Carbs: 10.2 g; Dietary Fiber: 0.7 g; Sugars: 6.7 g; Protein: 4.5 g; Cholesterol: 17 mg; Sodium: 21 mg

Virgin Sparkling Mojito

Yield: 1 Serving
Total Time: 5 Minutes
Prep Time: 5 Minutes
Cook Time: N/A

Ingredients

- Fresh mint leaves, crushed
- 6 ounces sparkling mineral water
- 2 tablespoons fresh lemon juice
- Peppermint stevia
- Crushed ice

Directions:

Mix all ingredients and serve garnished with mint.

Phase 3 modifications: Add a shot of rum.

Nutritional Information per Serving:

Calories: 5; Total Fat: 0 g; Carbs: 1 g; Dietary Fiber: 0.5 g; Sugars: 0 g; Protein: 0 g; Cholesterol: 0 mg; Sodium: 6 mg

Apple Green Tea Sparkler

Yield: 1 Serving
Total Time: 5 Minutes
Prep Time: 5 Minutes
Cook Time: N/A

Ingredients

- ½ cup brewed green tea, chilled
- 1 apple, juiced
- ¼ cup sparkling mineral water
- Pinch of cinnamon
- 1 teaspoon vanilla stevia

Directions:

Combine all ingredients and serve garnished with lemon wedge and apple curls.

Nutritional Information per Serving:

Calories: 117; Total Fat: 0.4 g; Carbs: 31 g; Dietary Fiber: 5.6 g; Sugars: 23.2 g; Protein: 0.2 g; Cholesterol: 0 mg; Sodium: 2 mg

Chocolate Toffee Coffee Smoothie

Yield: 1 Serving
Total Time: 5 Minutes
Prep Time: 5 Minutes
Cook Time: N/A

Ingredients

- 6 ounces brewed coffee
- 1 tablespoon milk
- ¼ teaspoon cocoa powder
- Dark or milk chocolate
- English toffee flavored
- Ice cubes

Directions:

Blend together all ingredients until smooth. Serve.

Phase 3 modifications: add cream or half and half.

Nutritional Information per Serving:

Calories: 48; Total Fat: 2.5 g; Carbs: 5.2 g; Dietary Fiber: 0.4 g; Sugars: 4.3 g; Protein: 1.3 g; Cholesterol: 0 mg; Sodium: 16 mg

Green Fruitea

Yield: 4 Servings

Total Time: 15 Minutes

Prep Time: 5 Minutes

Cook Time: 10 Minutes

Ingredients

- 1 cup boiled water
- 3 cups Water
- 1 cup fresh lemon Juice
- 5 bags Green Tea Single
- 4 drops flavored Stevia

Directions:

Bring water to a rolling boil; add tea bags and steep for about 4 minutes; strain tea into a pitcher and stir in more water, fresh lemon juice and stevia.

Nutritional Information per Serving:

Calories: 0; Total Fat: 0 g; Carbs: 0 g; Dietary Fiber: 0 g; Sugars: 0 g; Protein: 0 g; Cholesterol: 0 mg; Sodium: 12 mg

Sparkly Apple Tea

Yield: 1 Serving
Total Time: 5 Minutes
Prep Time: 5 Minutes
Cook Time: N/A

Ingredients

- Apple juice of 1 apple
- ½ cup green tea
- ¼ cup carbonated mineral water
- dash of nutmeg
- dash of cinnamon
- 1 teaspoon vanilla crème stevia

Directions:

Mix all the ingredients until well combined.

Nutritional Information per Serving:

Calories: 117; Total Fat: 0.4 g; Carbs: 31 g; Dietary Fiber: 5.6 g; Sugars: 23.2 g; Protein: 0.2 g; Cholesterol: 0 mg; Sodium: 2 mg

Fresh and Feisty Strawberry Lemonade

Yield: 1 Serving
Total Time: 5 Minutes
Prep Time: 5 Minutes
Cook Time: N/A

Ingredients

- 1 cup Strawberries
- ¼ cup fresh lemon juice
- 1 cup ice
- 10 drops plain stevia
- 10 drop lemon stevia

Directions:

Combine all ingredients in a blender and blend until smooth. Enjoy!

Nutritional Information per Serving:

Calories: 74; Total Fat: 0.7 g; Carbs: 17.8 g; Dietary Fiber: 4.6 g; Sugars: 11.4 g; Protein: 1.6 g; Cholesterol: 0 mg; Sodium: 2 mg

Sorbet 'de Strawberry

Yield: 1 serving
Total Time: 5 Minutes
Prep Time: 5 Minutes
Cook Time: N/A

Ingredients

- Handful Strawberries
- 1 lemon, peeled
- Water, as needed
- Stevia

Directions:

Freeze the strawberries for at least 1 hour; transfer to a blender and add in stevia, lemon, and water; blend until smooth. Freeze until firm, if desired. Enjoy!

Nutritional Information per Serving:

Calories: 54; Total Fat: 0.5 g; Carbs: 11.7 g; Dietary Fiber: 2.6 g; Sugars: 7.2 g; Protein: 1.1 g; Cholesterol: 0 mg; Sodium: 2 mg

Orange Strawberry Smoothie

Yield: 2 Servings
Total Time: 5 Minutes
Prep Time: 5 Minutes
Cook Time: N/A

Ingredients

- 1 cup frozen strawberries
- 1/3 cup fresh orange juice
- ¾ cup crushed ice
- 1 packet stevia
- handful spinach leaves, optional

Directions:

Blend together all ingredients in a blender until smooth. Enjoy!

Nutritional Information per Serving:

Calories: 87; Total Fat: 0.2 g; Carbs: 21.6 g; Dietary Fiber: 3.2 g; Sugars: 15.9 g; Protein: 0.6 g; Cholesterol: 0 mg; Sodium: 1 mg

Orange-Ade

Yield: 1 Serving
Total Time: 5 Minutes
Prep Time: 5 Minutes
Cook Time: N/A

Ingredients

- 1 Orange, peeled and sectioned
- Ice
- 8 drops vanilla crème Stevia
- Water, as needed

Directions:

In a blender, combine all ingredients and blend until smooth.

Nutritional Information per Serving:

Calories: 0; Total Fat: 0 g; Carbs: 0 g; Dietary Fiber: 0 g; Sugars: 0 g; Protein: 0 g; Cholesterol: 0 mg; Sodium: 10 mg

Parting Shot...

Eating a HCG diet is definitely one of the keys to the fountain of youth thanks to its fresh, healthy, natural, nutritious and wholesome food profile. Embark on this diet as soon as possible and you will star noticing distinct improvements in your appearance as well as energy levels. Start eating the HCG diet now for better health later.

Made in the USA
Columbia, SC
30 October 2024